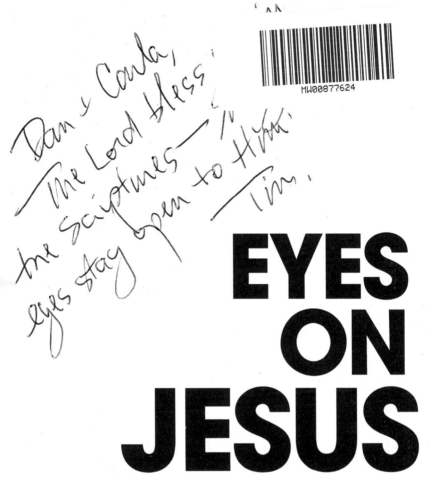

Dan & Carla,
The Lord bless
the Scriptures—
eyes stay open to Him.
Tim.

EYES
ON
JESUS

Through
Mark's Gospel

Tim MacIntosh

 FriesenPress

One Printers Way
Altona, MB R0G 0B0
Canada

www.friesenpress.com

ISBN
978-1-03-913893-3 (Hardcover)
978-1-03-913892-6 (Paperback)
978-1-03-913894-0 (eBook)

1. RELIGION, BIBLICAL MEDITATIONS

Distributed to the trade by The Ingram Book Company

for
Mom, who encouraged me to publish

for
Dad, who first modelled a love for the Scriptures

and for
Him to whom our eyes turn

GETTING STARTED

Eyes on Jesus.

That's the goal of the book you now hold in your hands. Our simple focus is to get to know Jesus better. We'll walk alongside him through the moments of his life, just as his disciples did two millennia ago. We'll see his actions (some of them startling), watch the expression on his face as he encounters people of all kinds, listen to his words (some spoken in anger, some in deep compassion, all of them instructive), and be drawn into his privileged inner circle. Do you want to come?

Through Mark's Gospel.

That's the path we'll journey. There's no better way to get eyes focused on Jesus than by reading through the Scriptures. I invite you to walk with me through one portion of Mark's Gospel each day. I'll provide some of my own reflections and you can then join me in a prayer. In addition, there will be some question or thought to ponder throughout the day.

Tradition tells us that Simon Peter was Mark's chief source for his writing. As we read, we'll have a front row seat to Jesus' life, because Peter himself was right there. So, read with anticipation. Hopefully this book helps on that journey. But please understand that the crucial component is actually reading Mark's words for yourself, written with the intent that we would see Jesus more clearly. So, read them. Don't bypass that step. Each section of this book begins with a reference to Mark's Gospel itself. Take the time to read what Mark wrote first.

It's a good adventure.

You can read these offerings at whatever pace you choose. But I suggest doing it five days per week, Monday to Friday. You can then take the weekends free to catch up, reflect further, catch your breath, memorize some verses, pray over what you've read, or however God leads. There's much grace in the process. If you get behind, don't worry. Just plunge in once again. Read. Reflect. Get to know Jesus.

One of the ongoing metaphors in this Gospel is that of open eyes and ears. After telling the parable of the Sower and the Seed, Jesus explained that the secret of the Kingdom of God was given to his followers, but those outside would be *ever seeing but never perceiving, and ever hearing but never understanding*" (Mark 4:12).

Jesus wants us to see. It's why he came. I invite you, through the gift of Mark's Gospel, to keep eyes on Jesus.

Come on the adventure.

MARK 1:1-8

The beginning of the gospel about Jesus Christ, the Son of God.

(verse 1)

Matthew, Mark, Luke, and John each give us a written account of the life and ministry of Jesus. These accounts are called Gospels, drawn from the Greek word that means *"good news,"* which of course is exactly what the whole story of Jesus is. Mark's version is the shortest, being concise, quick-moving, and action-packed, focusing less on Jesus' words (though they're certainly included) and more on the things he did.

In this fast-moving account, it's significant that Mark starts the way he does. Right in the first sentence he lays out for us the essence of Jesus' person, giving him two titles. He's the "Christ" (Greek translation of the Hebrew word *"Messiah"*), and also "Son of God." These are loaded phrases. We'll begin to unpack them in a moment.

But first, notice that right from the start Mark doesn't want us, in any way, to miss who Jesus is. Which is important because for most of the story, people just don't get it. Even the disciples, although having flashes of insight, don't seem to fully understand until after the resurrection. We, on the other hand, have the insider track. Mark wants us to see clearly, right from sentence one.

The first title, *"Christ,"* or *"Messiah,"* means *"Anointed One,"* the long-promised deliverer who would bring rescue and blessing to God's people. By Jesus' day, people fully expected a political

3

or military deliverance, especially in light of the current Roman occupation. They weren't prepared for a Messiah who would *"give his life as a ransom for many"* (Mark 10:45), so they didn't recognize who Jesus was.

Yet there's one breakthrough instance. It comes with Peter's insight in Mark 8:29, when he simply declares, *"You are the Christ."* So simple and straightforward. It's a central moment. The weight of the insight doesn't seem to stick with the disciples, but Mark wants it to stick with us. So he lays it out right at the start.

The second title, *"Son of God,"* was sometimes used of kings in the Old Testament, or even of the whole nation of Israel, but Mark uses it fully-loaded, implying someone who is uniquely divine. Jesus is God – don't miss it, Mark says.

But almost everyone in the unfolding story does. Apart from the Father in heaven calling Jesus his Son at his baptism and again at his Transfiguration, ironically, the only other insights come from unexpected sources. The first comes from evil spirits, who readily cry out, *"You are the Son of God"* (Mark 3:11 and 5:7), even though everyone else around fails to see it. The second comes from a non-Jewish Roman Centurion at the cross who, seeing the way Jesus died, declares, *"Surely this man was the Son of God"* (Mark 15:39). Again, no one else gets it. Mark, determined that we ourselves don't miss it, states it plainly right from the start.

So, keep your *eyes on Jesus* as this story unfolds. You won't hear these titles again often (because others in the story don't understand), but make sure you yourself keep the truth clearly in mind. This fast-paced story is going to give you sighting after sighting after sighting. Be ready to embrace them. Be ready to embrace him.

Dear Lord Jesus, give me eyes to see you clearly. In the simplicity of the story told in this Gospel, please let me simply see you. For your glory, and for my blessing. Amen.

Reflect:

If those who saw Jesus in person could so easily miss who he was, it's entirely possible for us to miss the reality of his active presence today, too. Keep your eyes open all day, watching for his activity. Name the sightings. Make yourself available.

MARK 1:9-13

At that time Jesus came from Nazareth in Galilee and was baptized by John in the Jordan. As Jesus was coming up out of the water, he saw heaven being torn open and the Spirit descending on him like a dove. And a voice came from heaven: "You are my Son, whom I love: with you I am well pleased."

At once the Spirit sent him out into the desert, and he was in the desert forty days, being tempted by Satan. He was with the wild animals, and angels attended him.

The quick flow of Mark's narrative makes for some interesting juxtapositions. Like here.

On the one hand, we have the Spirit's visible anointing and the Father's audible endorsement which, coming almost simultaneously, clearly set Jesus apart for any who have eyes to see and ears to hear. It's a transparent sighting of the reality of Jesus' spiritual life – he's empowered by the indwelling presence of the Spirit of God and embraced in an intimate, loving relationship with Almighty God.

Wouldn't you expect that to be the precursor to a season of peaceful bliss and spiritual blessing? Yet not so. *"At once"* the empowering Spirit sends him into the midst of a full-scale temptation-encounter with the devil. And it's not just momentary – it lasted forty days.

I find this instructive on so many levels.

1) Jesus himself is tempted. Mark doesn't bother recounting the nature of the temptation (you have to look at Matthew's or Luke's Gospels to get those details), but he certainly lets us know that Jesus experienced it. Which shouldn't, then, surprise me when I encounter temptation, too.

2) Being anointed with the Spirit doesn't keep one from temptation. Indeed, is it possible that the opposite is true?

3) What seems clear in this instance is that the intensity of spiritual blessing leads right into a season of spiritual battle. I shouldn't be surprised when I encounter the same.

4) Barren desert and wild animals perhaps provide a picture of the struggle of spiritual battle. It's not an easy place to be.

5) The battle can be prolonged. Jesus experienced forty days, one after another after another. Presumably Jesus knew that he hadn't failed just because the temptation didn't let up. I need to remember this for myself.

6) Jesus wasn't alone. He was anointed with the Spirit, in relationship with the Father, and attended by angels throughout this period of battle. Neither are we left alone – the Lord tells us: *"Never will I leave you; never will I forsake you"* (Heb. 13:5).

Jesus has been revealed to us as the Christ and the Son of God. We've watched as the Spirit has descended upon him and the Father's voice lovingly, approvingly echoed over him. Without skipping a beat, we now see him in the midst of temptation, full and strong.

Already we can see that this is a Saviour who is fully able, and one who meets us exactly where we are. Praise his name. As the story unfolds, keep eyes on him.

Lord Jesus, I honour you as the Spirit-anointed Son who is fully pleasing to the Father. Praise your name. I marvel at the intensity of the spiritual battle you have endured, emerging victorious. Praise your name. Open my eyes to see you fully and clearly. I submit to you as Lord.

———————

Reflect:

How can Jesus' experience of temptation equip and encourage you in the midst of your own moments (or seasons) of being tempted? Turn any insights into prayer – ask the Lord for his strength in the battle.

MARK 1:14-15

After John was put in prison, Jesus went into Galilee, proclaiming the good news of God. "The time has come," he said. "The kingdom of God is near. Repent and believe the good news!"

Mark's Gospel starts fast and furious. It's a breath-taking pace, covering in one chapter what both Matthew and Luke cover in four. The proclamation of John, Jesus' baptism, the temptation in the wilderness and the launch of a ministry of healing and deliverance are all here, all exploding on the scene.

At the centre is Jesus' announcement of the good news, a declaration that gives meaning to all the rest. *"The time is now* – here it is," the words sounding a drum-roll of anticipation. *"The kingdom of God is near."*

"Near" gives the sense that it's not quite here in all its fullness, but not distant either. Indeed, right at the door; in fact, breaking in! The very presence and kingly rule of God, long yearned for, is breaking into human experience in the person of Jesus himself.

Mark lets us graphically see this in-breaking Kingdom by its impact on individual lives – the man released from demonic possession, Simon's mother-in-law restored from debilitating fever, sicknesses healed, demons banished, and a leprous man beautifully cleansed of his disease. The Kingdom is near! Indeed, breaking in.

The response Jesus calls for is also the ongoing call to us. *"Repent and believe the good news!"* Of course. *"Repent"* means to have a change of mind that leads to a change of behaviour, a full reorientation of life to God. It's the call to conversion, yes, but an ongoing call to keep turning away from the things that distract (*"putting off,"* in Paul's language) and turning toward God (*"putting on,"* as Paul would say), steering into the stream of his kingly rule.

"Believe" means more than intellectual assent. It's throwing in your lot with the Master, staking your life on him. Jesus' subsequent call to the fishermen gives it more feet-on-the-ground expression: *"Come, follow me" (verse 17).* Live, step by step, in the full reality of God's Kingdom, here, now, in the lordship of Jesus.

The urgency and excitement and fast-paced movement of this chapter is meant to draw us in. *Repent* – keep turning toward the King. *Believe* – let every moment be infused with Kingdom awareness. *Follow* – express that Kingdom commitment with step-by-step obedience.

Join the adventure. That's Mark's message.

Dear Lord Jesus, I welcome your presence. I am glad, so glad, of your Kingdom rule. I turn again into the stream of your lordship. I reorient myself to view this day as an expression of your purpose and rule. I offer myself as a follower, watching your lead.

Live your life in me. O Lord.

Eyes open:
Be alert this day for moments that need the intervention of the Kingdom. Take Jesus' prayer, *"Your Kingdom come, your will be done,"* praying it over each of those moments as you encounter them.

MARK 1:16-20

As Jesus walked beside the Sea of Galilee, he saw Simon and his brother Andrew casting a net into the lake, for they were fishermen. "Come, follow me," Jesus said, "and I will send you out to fish for people." At once they left their nets and followed him.
(verses 16–18)

This isn't the first time Simon and Andrew meet Jesus. John 1:35–42 gives us an earlier encounter, likely also involving John, one of the sons of Zebedee. On that occasion Jesus gave Simon a nickname – "Peter," meaning "Rock." The name stuck, though it took Simon much longer to actually live into its connotation.

Mark leaves all that out and simply cuts to the chase, giving us the moment when Jesus calls these two brothers to commitment. *"Come, follow me."*

Such a simple command. But so decisive and costly, as we see from their response. They left their nets, encompassing their livelihood and former career path, and stepped forward to follow Jesus. Such "following" implies fixing eyes on him rather than on one's own goals and aspirations. It requires active engagement, putting one foot in front of the other, rather than just mental assent to a new ideal. It means using those feet to go where Jesus himself is going, and using one's hands to do what Jesus is doing. It means keeping up with his pace, submitting to his lead, lingering where he lingers, staying focused where he's focused. All of this was probably unsettling for fishermen who kept their own schedule and submitted only to wind and waves.

In the process of it all, Jesus has transformation in view. He's going to remake Simon and Andrew and any others who choose to join the journey. The NIV translation (above) translates Jesus as saying, *"I will send you out to fish for people."* It's a reasonable translation, giving us the main point, but a more literal translation is better. *"Send"* implies that Jesus simply gives a directive and expects compliance. What Mark literally writes is actually more supportive and involved. *"I will make you become fishers"* – that's the literal wording. I love it, because it captures the fullness of the process. Jesus commits himself to doing a work of transformation in these guys, enabling them to carry out the very task he is assigning them. He doesn't simply command. No, he re-shapes them, the responsibility being in his own hands to effect the transformation. *"I will make you become."*.

There is such hope for us, too. The tasks our Lord calls us to, mission included, are ones he equips us to carry out. Transformation guaranteed. Indeed, it's sometimes in the very context of us stepping forward to follow him that some of his best work is accomplished in our lives. We may feel completely ill-equipped in the face of his calling. We may find ourselves initially entirely out of our depth. But his words still ring out, as they did at Galilee. *"I will make you become."*

Oh, yes – carry it out, O Lord!

Lord Jesus, I am listening for your call. Some of it I've heard already. But I'm ready for more. In it all, I choose to submit to your transforming work. I need it. I welcome it. Even so, come, Lord Jesus.

Reflect:
What call have you heard from Jesus? What transformation is needed? Will you trust him to do what needs to be done? Tell him. Submit to his work.

MARK 1:21-28

They went to Capernaum, and when the Sabbath came, Jesus went into the synagogue and began to teach. The people were amazed at his teaching, because he taught them with authority, not as the teachers of the law. Just then a man in their synagogue who was possessed by an evil spirit cried out, "What do you want with us, Jesus of Nazareth? Have you come to destroy us? I know who you are – the Holy One of God!"

"Be quiet!" said Jesus sternly. "Come out of him!" The evil spirit shook the man violently and came out of him with a shriek.

The people were all so amazed that they asked each other, "What is this? A new teaching – and with authority! He even gives orders to evil spirits and they obey him."

(verses 21–27)

Authority. This is the key word in this passage. As soon as Jesus begins to teach, the people hear it.

What was it they heard? I imagine it was a certain settled, straightforward confidence in the way Jesus presented truth – a certain power of conviction that permeated his words. He spoke like he knew what he was talking about. After all, this is the One who called worlds into being, who simply said, *"Let there be light,"* and there was light (Col. 1:16). Imagine hearing that same voice speaking out loudly and clearly in your very presence. No wonder they sat up and took notice.

By comparison, the teachers of the law were at a clear disadvantage. We might fault them for not "teaching with authority." But how could they possibly compare? They had the law, but they were one step removed, only being recipients, and doing their best to receive it well and truly. But here, now, was the Giver himself, the One from whose mind and heart and will the very teaching originated. How could the scribes possibly compete? No wonder the people sat up and took notice.

And then an oppressive spirit, resident in the life of one of those present, sat up and took notice also. "What do you want with us, Jesus of Nazareth?" the voice croaked out. "I know who you are – the Holy One of God!" But that voice of evil was out-gunned by the voice of Light. "Be quiet!" Jesus demanded. The voice whose command had released light into darkness, now shut up darkness within silence, declaring, "Be muzzled – be reduced to silence! Come out of him!"

Again, authority rang out. Again, the people heard. Loud and clear. And the effect was obvious. Immediate. There was a violent shaking, a loud shrieking, and the man was released.

No wonder the people noticed. Both Jesus' teaching and his actions echoed with authority. Amazement was the result. "The people were amazed at his teaching . . . The people were all so amazed . . ." It was a good beginning, and Jesus himself is patient with the pace of our slowly dawning realizations. But, ultimately, amazement isn't enough. The only appropriate response to authority has to be much weightier. It's to own him as Lord. To give him our will. To yield to him our obedience. To follow him with all we've got.

Like those first disciples responding to the authoritative command, "Follow me," by leaving boats and fishing nets behind. Even then, they were in for a steep learning curve.

Lord Jesus, I acknowledge your authority over all Creation, speaking worlds into being and commanding light in the darkness. I acknowledge the authority of your teaching and commands, your Kingdom and your will. I welcome your authority right here, right now. Strengthen me to follow. For your glory.

———————

Reflect:

Praise him for his lordship. Pause to submit yourself afresh. As you do, ask him: Lord, is there any place in my life you want to further your authority? Then ask yourself: Is there anything holding me back from submitting to him there?

MARK 1:29-34

That evening after sunset the people brought to Jesus all the sick and demon-possessed. The whole town gathered at the door, and Jesus healed many who had various diseases. He also drove out many demons . . .

(verses 32–34)

"*The time has come. The kingdom of God is near*" (Mark 1:15). Jesus had begun his preaching ministry with these words. Now he is demonstrating the reality of the Kingdom's nearness.

Isaiah had prophesied what it would be like when "*your God will come . . . he will come to save you*" (Isa. 35:4). The blind will see, the deaf hear, the lame walk (indeed "*leap like a deer*"!), and the dumb talk – and those imprisoned will be set free. On the doorstep of Simon Peter's house, the signs of the Kingdom are now being played out in technicolour.

I love the fact that Jesus begins so simply and practically inside the home with the healing of Simon's mother-in-law. We don't know the severity of her illness, only that she was confined to bed. Certainly it was not as obvious a malady as blindness, deafness, or lameness. But it incapacitated this woman and disrupted the household. Jesus sets it right, restoring her to health, releasing her from the bonds of fever, and allowing her to step back fully into life and productivity.

Somehow the word spread. Did Simon's children dash out into the streets, excitedly celebrating Grandma's healing? We don't

17

know. But people heard and, knowing their own need, they came. All those who were sick and demon-possessed came. Mark says the whole town gathered at the door. And Jesus healed them.

What a wonderful image, Jesus framed in the doorway as dusk deepened and light from lamps inside the house spilled forth. Just as he'd restored Simon's mother-in-law, he now *"healed many who had various diseases."* Nothing stood in the way. Nothing was insurmountable. Not even the invisible presence of demonic forces who afflicted many. Mark tells us that Jesus *"drove them out,"* using a word that implies violent forcefulness. The Kingdom has come decisively near.

Our Lord would later teach us to pray, *"Your kingdom come, your will be done on earth as it is in heaven"* (Matt. 6:10). It might help to bear this scene in mind as we follow this instruction, glimpsing the health and happy bustle of a restored household, light spilling forth from the doorway into the fading day, and Jesus standing front and centre, with compassion in his eyes and authority in his person, reversing the impact of brokenness and evil. With Jesus here, the Kingdom is near. Anything is possible.

Lord, with this scene in mind, I pray, "Your Kingdom come, your will be done here, as in heaven." I bring to you now the needs of the world around me – gathering each one before you. I bring to you my own needs. Thank you that you stand ready. Praise you that you are able. I wait on your Kingdom-touch.

Pray:
Take the above prayer and pray it now, filling it with people and circumstances and needs from your own circle. Look to Jesus. Wait on him.

MARK 1:35-39

Very early in the morning, while it was still dark, Jesus got up, left the house and went off to a solitary place, where he prayed. Simon and his companions went to look for him, and when they found him, they exclaimed: "Everyone is looking for you!" Jesus replied, "Let us go somewhere else – to the nearby villages – so I can preach there also. That is why I have come." So he traveled throughout Galilee, preaching in their synagogues and driving out demons.

Anchored in the midst of these fast-paced opening episodes of Jesus' ministry is this early morning scene of solitude. Already we have experienced Jesus' power and authority, conviction and passion. Here, we are returned to his foundation. We've heard the Father speak affirmation and love over his Son. Here we see the Son anchored in that relationship.

Interestingly, Mark gives us only two other scenes of Jesus praying, but this instance, coming right in the throes of his emerging ministry, sets the pattern.

We don't know the content of Jesus' prayer, but we see its effect. The beginning band of disciples, with Simon in the lead, intrude on Jesus' solitude with the compelling news that he is receiving acclaim, the crowds clamouring for his presence. But Jesus is clear in his calling. He's received his marching orders from the Father. He knows his priority, because he knows his commitment to doing what he sees his Father doing.

Of course, Jesus is the Son of God, as Mark has made clear right off the top. He is deeply (eternally) aware that he has been sent into the world on mission. *"The Son of Man came to seek and to save the lost"* (Luke 19:10). He wouldn't forget. He couldn't. Nor would he forget his relationship with the Father. *"I and the Father are one,"* he would tell the crowds (John 10:30). The awareness was part of his very being. The connection was constant, vibrant, vital. It couldn't be broken.

But he nurtured the relationship through continual communion. Slipping away in the pre-dawn darkness, he carved out space and time. Every moment would already have been filled with conscious connection to the Father and deep awareness of the Spirit's presence. And yet, he took the time aside. He found a place alone. Deliberately.

So, I ask myself, if Jesus felt the need, what about me? If the eternal Son of God chose to take time in hand, setting it aside for prayer, how can I not? Oh, how I need to remove distraction. To focus on my Lord. To sense his presence. To seek his guidance. To hear his voice. Oh, how I need time in prayer.

So, with eyes on Jesus, I follow him again to that solitary place. There may be many other voices. Challenges may be pressing in. Opportunities may be unfolding before me. But I choose the solitude, for this time, setting the clamour aside, entering the place of communion once again.

Jesus has gone before. All is ready. The time is here.

Lord Jesus, thank you for your example. You have gone before me. Help me now. Your promise is sure: Draw near to God and he will draw near to you. Thank you.

Pray:
Take the time, right now. Enter in. Pray.

MARK 1:40-45

A man with leprosy came to him and begged him on his knees,
"If you are willing, you can make me clean."
Filled with compassion, Jesus reached out his hand and touched
the man. "I am willing," he said. "Be clean!" Immediately the
leprosy left him and he was cured.
(verses 40–42)

Faith and desperation. That's what I see in this man. Helplessly afflicted with leprosy, he regularly had to declare it to the world as he cleared the way in front of him, calling out, "Unclean! Unclean!" He was isolated, cut off from human contact and barred from the worshipping community.

Put yourself in the man's position. As he falls to his knees, completely vulnerable before Jesus, what is he saying? It strikes me that he's crying out in sheer desperation. He's declaring with the whole of his being: *Here I plant myself. I have no other hope. I'm laid bare before you, Master. All my options are exhausted. I put myself completely in your hands. I'm powerless.*

Desperation, yes. But not despair. Instead, faith. Somehow, he knows enough about Jesus to spark hope. Had he heard about the evening outside the doorway in Capernaum where diseases of all kinds were healed? Had he heard stories of dramatic deliverances from evil that accompanied Jesus' preaching? Somehow, he knows Jesus is able. It crystallizes into faith. In desperation, he puts it into

21

words: *"If you are willing, you can make me clean."* Convinced of Jesus' power, he submits to Jesus' will, and his goodness.

On the edge of our seats, before we hear Jesus' response, Mark pulls back the curtain and gives us an inside view. Jesus, we're told, is *"filled with compassion."* This is one of my favourite Greek words. The word is *splanchnizomai*, coming from the root word *splanchna*, which simply means "guts." This word (*splanchnizomai*) is the verbal form that speaks of a deep-seated response of compassion, welling up from the very depths of a person's being – right from their guts. What a graphic word to use of Jesus. What an amazing wonder that it's true.

As the man lies prone at his feet, Jesus feels deep compassion. *"If you are willing,"* the man had said – tentatively, hoping to the very depths of his own being that Jesus would be. He waits. And now the words come forth from Jesus' mouth, spoken with *splanchnizomai*. These simple, powerful words: *"I am willing."*

If nothing more was spoken, if nothing more was done, this would be enough to change the man's life forever. Ever after, he would be able to live in that truth, that Jesus (whom Mark has already told us is *Christ* and *Son of God*, and therefore the Sovereign Lord), feels for him, has compassion on him, and expresses he is on-side with him – *"I am willing."*

But the words don't stop there. *"Be clean!"* Jesus says. And the man is transformed. The leprosy is gone, in an instant.

None of us have had the opportunity, as this man had, to meet Jesus physically on the road, or to throw ourselves at his feet, or to hear the timbre of his voice as he says, *"I am willing. Be clean!"* But equally powerfully, we have the opportunity to see, to hear, to experience the deep-seated compassion, and to know the immediate cleansing, through and through.

It's the cross. There, the deep compassion of Jesus was unmistakably made known. His eternal willingness to provide cleansing was forever made clear. Life-changing washing, healing, cleansing was brought about for all who accept by faith.

Desperation and faith. What a glorious combination – if we encounter Jesus.

———————

Lord Jesus, thank you that what this man experienced is also true for me – your compassion, your willingness, your healing touch, your full cleansing work. All of it provided at the cross. Thank you.

———————

Reflect:
Even once we've received Jesus' cleansing work, there are times we need to know its depth once again. If this is one of those times, meditate on the story: know Jesus' compassion, hear his willingness, experience his touch, receive his transforming word of cleansing. Give thanks.

MARK 2:1–12

Some men came, bringing to him a paralytic, carried by four of them. Since they could not get him to Jesus because of the crowd, they made an opening in the roof above Jesus and, after digging through it, lowered the mat the paralyzed man was lying on. When Jesus saw their faith, he said to the paralytic, "Son, your sins are forgiven . . . I tell you, get up, take your mat and go home." He got up, took his mat and walked out in full view of them all. This amazed everyone and they praised God, saying, "We have never seen anything like this!"
(verses 3–5, 11–12)

This story gives us a clear sighting of faith. It also gives us the first instance of controversy and opposition to Jesus, which continues to emerge, like weeds in a garden, for the rest of this chapter, carrying through to Jesus' trial and crucifixion much later. This opposition provides the stark counterpoint to faith, making faith shine the brighter.

The background to the story is the doorstep of Simon's house, right there in Capernaum. At that location, just a short time before, many people had gathered hoping for healing and deliverance by the hands of Jesus. And they received it. Jesus has now returned and the crowd has re-gathered (perhaps at Simon's house again?) – they've come readily and eagerly because of what they'd previously seen. They fill the house and jam the doorway.

Has faith brought these individuals together? It's not yet clear. At the end of the episode we're told that everyone assembled was amazed at the miraculous healing, so much so that they praised God, saying, *"We have never seen anything like this!"* But is "amazement" faith? Not necessarily. Mark comments often in his narrative that people were amazed or astonished by Jesus. We've seen it twice already in the previous chapter as the people in this same town of Capernaum listened to his teaching in the synagogue and watched as he delivered a man from an evil spirit (Mark 1:21–28) – at each point they were *"amazed"* at his authority. But they don't quite apprehend who Jesus is. The evil spirit actually cries it out. But the people don't. Amazement may often be a pathway to faith, but it doesn't necessarily get you all the way there.

In contrast, we've got the four friends, ropes in hand, lowering their buddy from the ceiling right into Jesus' line of sights. Mark clearly tells us that Jesus looks at them and perceives faith. He'd be the one to know! This is the first time Mark mentions the word in his account. The forgiveness and healing are going to be received by the paralyzed man himself. But Jesus sees faith in the four friends.

What was it he saw? Presumably there were eager eyes looking down through the newly opened hole in the ceiling, focusing alternately on the immobilized man on the mat and on Jesus, who held all their hope. Presumably, he'd seen the effort it took to open the ceiling in the first place, bits of ceiling and roofing material drifting down in the process. With the ceiling open, he saw arms flexing and fists clenching as the men worked the ropes, lowering their friend inch by inch, hope by hope, into Jesus' very presence. All of this may have been sparked by amazement in the synagogue at Jesus' authority, or by astonishment on Simon's doorstep as they encountered healing after healing. But faith was crystallized as they took the active step of putting their friend and his need right in front of Jesus.

25

I often think of faith (in contrast to mere intellectual assent) as putting the weight of our lives in Jesus' hands alone. Here, these men literally lower the weight of their friend's life right into Jesus' presence, trusting he will act. It's faith, pure and simple.

That's what I want.

———

Lord Jesus, I acknowledge you are able. I stand in awe of your deeds. Strengthen my faith and determination to bring every need into your presence. Especially, may I be one who faithfully grabs hold of a friend's need and boldly brings it to you. Help me, Lord.

———

Pray:
Think of a friend's weighty need. Use this image of the hole in the roof, and the ropes, and the mat. Through prayer, lower your friend right into the very presence of Jesus. With eyes on them, acknowledge all their need. With eyes on Jesus, entrust it all to him.

MARK 2:13-17

*As he walked along, he saw Levi son of Alphaeus sitting at
the tax collector's booth. "Follow me," Jesus told him,
and Levi got up and followed him.*

*While Jesus was having dinner at Levi's house, many tax collec-
tors and "sinners" were eating with him and his disciples,
for there were many who followed him . . .*

*"It is not the healthy who need a doctor, but the sick. I have
not come to call the righteous, but sinners."*

(verses 14–15, 17)

---

*Thank you so much, Lord Jesus, that you have come as a doctor for
the sick, rather than dispensing "good housekeeping seals" for righteousness. Were that the case, I would fail. As would we all.*

There were probably few people in the vicinity that day who were
as despised as Levi. Tax collectors were Roman collaborators,
making their livelihood by overcharging those they taxed. Not a
commendable profession. Levi was certainly despised. Yet Jesus
makes no secret of calling him as a follower, and then very publicly goes to dinner at his house, alongside many of Levi's friends.

This earned Jesus the accusation of being *"the friend of tax collectors and sinners"* (Matt. 11:19). It's a true insight. It's a glorious
title. And it provides such deep assurance of grace. He came to

seek and to save the lost – that's me. He came for the sick, not the self-healed – me again. It wasn't those with righteous credentials, but rather those without any claim to holiness – those were the ones on whom he set his sights.

O Lord, thank you – it's me.

I see in this story such warm embrace, Jesus moving right into Levi's company. Levi opened the door and Jesus stepped straight in, before Levi ever had a chance to clean house, to change profession, to straighten up his act, or sort out his friendships.

In real-time, in narrative form, this is exactly what Paul tells us in theological terms. *"While we were still sinners . . . when we were God's enemies, we were reconciled to him through the death of his Son"* (Rom. 5:8, 10). Jesus paid the price. He came the distance. He embraced sinners as friends. Including me.

Lord Jesus, thank you for this picture of your embracing heart, revealed at a despised tax booth and sinner's dinner table. Thank you that you came with your sight set on sinners, your sight set on me. I hear your knock. I open the door once again gladly – come in.

Reflect:
Take time, right now, to welcome Jesus afresh. Don't tidy up first. Let him embrace you right where you are. Then, heeding his voice, choose to follow more closely yet.

MARK 2:18-22

Jesus answered, "How can the guests of the bridegroom fast while he is with them? They cannot, so long as they have him with them. But the time will come when the bridegroom will be taken away from them, and on that day they will fast."
(verses 19-20)

Fasting is a gift given by God. It's a discipline of the spiritual life that can be used in repentance, intercession, worship, and seeking guidance. We see Paul and Barnabas and other leaders of the church in Antioch engaging in worship and fasting that led to new insight and direction from the Lord. What a gift.

In the Old Testament, fasting was mandated annually on the Day of Atonement. Later, other regular days of fasting were added, for the sake of repentance, prompting a fresh turning to the Lord. How good.

The benefit of fasting is its physicality – it's an outward expression that effects our body (and comfort level) as we experience the craving for food. Hunger becomes part of our spiritual connection with the Lord.

But that physicality can also become fasting's danger. Since it's such a tangible, obvious discipline, it's possible to pridefully see it as spiritual achievement, embracing it as a sign, for ourselves and others, of the depth of our religious commitment. This seems to be what happened to the Pharisees. They had taken up the practice of twice weekly fasts, allowing themselves to look wan and unkempt so others would know. They legalistically established it as the expected standard of spirituality. It was part of their ongoing sense of rigidity.

Further, they seem to have embraced fasting in hopes of hastening the coming of Messiah and establishing God's Kingdom. Certainly this was the perspective of the rabbis in succeeding generations – they thought if the nation would make itself ready by religious observance, fasting included, Messiah would come. So, mournfully, they fasted week by week.

And they wanted everyone to do the same.

But Jesus bursts through this rigid, mournful gloom. When asked why his disciples don't fast like those of the Pharisees, he joyfully responds, "The bridegroom is here!" Of course. You don't fast at a wedding feast! It's time for celebration, not mourning.

We've had weddings for two of our kids so far. Both were amazing celebrations. One was far away, so we had a vacation. The other was close at hand, so people travelled to us! Both involved good food, music, excitement, and lots and lots of visiting. There were family and new in-laws, plus important friends from both sides. There were speeches and joyful tears and raucous laughter.

But neither event would have been anything at all without the bride and groom. Amid all the joy, they were the centre. Their presence made the party. Without them, it would have been a bust.

Jesus is the bridegroom. His presence makes all the difference. He welcomes us into relationship – we share his joy. He calls us friends. How could we head back into gloom.

Oh, there would come a time when the disciples would experience grief from his absence – the cross brought that cruelly to pass. But, as Jesus told his disciples in advance, *"after a little while you will see me . . . and you will rejoice, and no one will take away your joy"* (John 16:17, 22).

When, in later days, the early church engaged in fasting, it was infused with a new awareness – the joy of his presence.

The bridegroom has come. The Kingdom is breaking in.

Lord Jesus, I receive the joy of your presence. Thank you for drawing me into your circle, into your gladness.

Reflect:

"The joy of the Lord is your strength," says Nehemiah (8:10). Remind yourself throughout the day of his continuing presence – renew the joy.

MARK 2:23-28

One Sabbath Jesus was going through the grainfields, and as his disciples walked along, they began to pick some heads of grain. The Pharisees said to him, "Look, why are they doing what is unlawful on the Sabbath?" . . .

Then he said to them, "The Sabbath was made for man, not man for the Sabbath. So the Son of Man is Lord even of the Sabbath."

(verses 23–24, 27–28)

So much of the Pharisees' view of life and godliness seems to have been shaped by a very constrained view of God himself, seeing him as some kind of celestial traffic cop whose chief focus is watching for infractions.

Certainly this influenced their view of Sabbath-keeping. "Restriction" was the key word defining "Sabbath" in their vocabulary. Over time they had tightened the constraints more and more, adding increasingly specific restrictions, in an effort to keep people from infringing on the Sabbath commandment. Ultimately the rabbis mandated thirty-nine specific kinds of work activity that were outlawed. It was as if they saw themselves as traffic-cops-in-training, whistles and "Do Not Enter" signs in hand, erecting successive layers of barricade to keep unsuspecting motorists back from a major sinkhole.

It was a completely tainted view of Sabbath, which had not originally been given for the purpose of restrictive constraint, but rather as blessing. The word itself means *"rest."* It was God's good

32

gift to his people. Work comes on the other days of the week, often in a non-stop flow in an agrarian culture (and seemingly equally so in many spheres of modern life). But God gave the Sabbath commandment to provide release and refreshment. Rest.

Keeping the Sabbath was, of course, also a very tangible way of honouring the Lord. Even when surrounding cultures and economies took no break, God's people were called in obedience to do so, trusting the Lord with the consequences. But the law itself was not given for constraint, but blessing.

"The Sabbath was made for man, not man for the Sabbath." So when the Pharisees applied one of their Sabbath strictures ("Do Not Reap") to the disciples' innocent act of picking grain to satisfy hunger, they were completely missing the point. Sabbath was always meant as blessing.

Indeed, Jesus pushes the issue further by recounting, with approval, the story of David taking the priests-only consecrated bread from the Tabernacle to feed his hungry men. Meeting real human need seems to be in line with the heart of God.

Ultimately, the bottom line in this whole encounter comes with the realization that these Pharisees are sounding off at the very One who gave the commandment in the first place.

"So the Son of Man is Lord even of the Sabbath." Look to him for guidance. Come to him for rest. Find in him blessing that brings freedom and refreshment.

Dear Lord Jesus, praise you that you are Lord even of the Sabbath. You command rest for your people. You bestow grace. Conform my thinking to be in line with your own. Make me a channel of grace to those in need, a champion of freedom to those falsely constrained.

Reflect:

Submit your own thinking afresh to the Lord. Are there any constraints (or judgements or legalisms) you have placed on others? Ask the Lord for his perspective.

MARK 3:1-6

Another time he went into the synagogue and a man with a shriveled hand was there. Some of them were looking for a reason to accuse Jesus, so they watched him closely to see if he would heal him on the Sabbath. Jesus said to the man with the shriveled hand, "Stand up in front of everyone."

Then Jesus asked them, "Which is lawful on the Sabbath: to do good or to do evil, to save life or to kill?" But they remained silent.

He looked around at them in anger and, deeply distressed at their stubborn hearts, said to the man, "Stretch out your hand." He stretched it out, and his hand was completely restored. Then the Pharisees went out and began to plot with the Herodians how they might kill Jesus.

From the beginning of Chapter 2 to this point we have encountered growing hostility and opposition to Jesus. At each step along the way, religious leaders have found offense in Jesus' words and deeds and attitudes. Finally it culminates here in active plotting to end Jesus' life. And we're only at the beginning of Chapter 3!

How did these guys get it so wrong? With Jesus right in front of them, how did they remain so blind to his person and his purposes? Why can't they see Jesus for who he is?

Here are some things I notice about the Pharisees:

- They don't share Jesus' perspective. The man with the shriveled hand comes on the scene, but there is no indication whatsoever of compassion on their part. We know explicitly from Jesus' encounter with the leprous man (Mark 1:40–45) that he himself feels deep compassion for such people. But the Pharisees only view the man as effective bait in a trap for Jesus.

- They're looking for fault. They enter into this moment *"looking for a reason to accuse Jesus."* Their perception is pre-determined. They can't see anything else.

- They have an unassailably legalistic worldview. Their view of the Sabbath is ironclad and unshakable. They don't perceive it as a gift of God-given rest, but rather as a confining barrier. Healing is not allowed. Eagerly, they watch Jesus *"closely to see if he would heal on the Sabbath."*

- They can't hear reason. Jesus, by his question, points out that the Sabbath is meant for good. Their minds are made up – they can't hear it.

- They can't see the signs. Jesus works a clear miracle before their very eyes. The man's outstretched hand is transformed. It must have been remarkable to see – the withered limb expanding with muscle, stretching with health, the joint gaining flexibility and the hand visibly growing in strength. But when they see it, they miss it. They're filled with fury instead.

Meanwhile, we find Jesus himself angry for different reasons. All that we've just reviewed distresses him deeply, for he sees their thickly calloused hearts.

But neither the opposition nor his own anger deter him from caring for the man who is before him. He brings healing to him so that he is *"completely restored."*

The Son of Man, who is Lord of the Sabbath, releases life and goodness that ripple outward, from fingers and hand and limb, into new possibilities and freedom for this man. Meanwhile, the Pharisees cling to their own view of the Sabbath, hatching murderous conspiracies in the process. The sighting of Jesus is growing clearer and clearer.

Lord Jesus, thank you that you see our need. Thank you that you extend life and salvation, healing and freedom. I receive you as Lord of the Sabbath.

Reflect:

At what points am I blind to the heart and purposes of Jesus? Is there a person or situation before me today that I need to rethink from Jesus' perspective?

MARK 3:7-12

Whenever the evil spirits saw him, they fell down before him and cried out, "You are the Son of God." But he gave them strict orders not to tell who he was.

(verses 11–12)

In his first letter, the Apostle John writes, *"The reason the Son of God appeared was to destroy the devil's work"* (1 John 3:8). That task was decisively accomplished at the cross. But clearly the forces of evil were threatened by Jesus' presence right from the start. They understood why he'd come. They cowered before him.

The first time an evil spirit makes an appearance in Mark's Gospel, it cries out, *"What do you want with us, Jesus of Nazareth? Have you come to destroy us?"* (Mark 1:24). Having stated its fear, it went on to declare, *"I know who you are – the Holy One of God."* Here in Mark 3, the declaration of Jesus' identity seems to be undergirded by that same sense of fearful trepidation.

No wonder they were afraid. Destruction was coming. But why did they cry out his name? Why did they declare his awesome identity? Some suggest it was connected with the belief of occult-practitioners that pronouncing the precise name of a person yielded control over them. If that's the case, these spirits were slow learners, for time and again Jesus remained undaunted. Perhaps, instead, these spirits were simply voicing terrified surprise when finding themselves face to face with the Lord of all; as if rounding a corner, they were caught off guard by his majesty, declaring his name in sheer astonishment: *"You are the Son of God!"*

Whatever the reason, it's clear these spiritual scourges know they are completely outgunned by Jesus. Indeed, one of the hallmarks of his ministry was confrontation with these powers of darkness. Early in his account, Mark simply states, *"He also drove out many demons"* (1:34). And it was one of the key tasks Jesus gave his disciples when he sent them out, equipping them with *"authority to drive out demons"* (3:15). The Kingdom of God was breaking into the kingdom of darkness. Or, putting it the other way around, as Paul does later, it is through Jesus that God *"has rescued us from the dominion of darkness and brought us into the Kingdom of the Son he loves"* (Col. 1:14).

As to why Jesus gave *"strict orders not to tell who he was"* (verse 12), it seems he realized people would only misunderstand his identity until they could see it through the cross. They would expect a King, without the suffering. They would expect a Deliverer, without the sacrifice. They would expect glory, without the shame. Later, when coming down from the Mount of Transfiguration with Peter and James and John, all three having seen his glory on the mountain, he gave them orders, also, not to tell what they'd seen *"until the Son of Man had risen from the dead"* (Mark 9:9). In other words, not until after the cross. The cross would be the place of deliverance. It would spell the destruction of the forces of evil. But it would come at a cost. His own life, laid down, would be the price. That sacrifice was the measure of his person.

"The reason the Son of God appeared was to destroy the devil's work." The demons knew it. They trembled with fear. But we, by faith, receive its finished impact, the work of Christ which provides salvation. Oh, there's still more deliverance for him to work in our lives, each step along the way. There are ongoing battles yet with the forces of darkness, until that great future day when the Lord returns and sets everything to rights. But right now, through

faith, we ourselves cry out with full clarity and truth, *"You are the Son of God!"*

And we rejoice.

Dear Lord Jesus, thank you that you have destroyed the works of the enemy. I receive your salvation with joy. Praise you that you are the Sovereign Lord. Indeed, you are the Son of God. I declare it and rejoice.

Reflect:

Take time right now to pray the prayer he gave us: *"Lead us not into temptation, but deliver us from evil."* Place into his hands your own trials and struggles. Rejoice – he is Lord.

MARK 3:13-19 (PART 1)

*Jesus went up on a mountainside and called to him those
he wanted, and they came to him. He appointed twelve –
designating them apostles – that they might be with him and
that he might send them out to preach and to have
authority to drive out demons.*

(verses 13–15)

So much here in these few short verses. This portion is steeped in the prayerful solitude of Mark 1:35–39 – Mark doesn't tell us, but Luke does. Jesus went to that mountainside to pray, praying all night to the Father, then, when morning came, calling his disciples together and choosing twelve to be *"apostles."* The name itself literally means *"sent ones,"* anticipating one key part of the calling he is about to unfold for them.

But first things first. The foundational aspect of this calling was *"that they might be with him"* (verse 14). They were to be drawn into relationship with the Master, indeed, into friendship, as Jesus himself would later say (John 15:14–15). This undergirds everything. In knowing Jesus, these apostles were being nurtured in the moment-by-moment reality of abiding, like a branch in the vine, a relationship that would later be infused and maintained by the indwelling presence of the very Spirit of Jesus, so that they would never be left alone, never orphaned. This vital foundation, modelled by them, has been passed on to us. Our chief calling, too, is to be with the One who has come to be *"God with us,"* to

41

fill us with his Spirit's presence that we might live in continuing connection with the One who calls us friend.

This was the atmosphere. Then came the activity. They were to be *"sent."* Mark characterizes this mission as encompassing two things: preaching and casting out demons.

"Preaching" doesn't necessarily imply a pulpit. Fundamentally it means to proclaim or declare the good news of the Kingdom – the good news of Jesus himself. It may not come with great eloquence, but those who have spent time with Jesus will simply spill forth the good news. I'm reminded of the quote attributed to St Francis of Assisi: *"Preach the gospel at all times, and when necessary, use words."* In other words, with the whole of who we are, both in word and deed, make Jesus known. Don't hold back. This, we have been sent to do.

But there's more. The disciples were also sent with authority to cast out demons. They had seen this from front row seats in Jesus' ministry, dramatic moments when Jesus himself routed forces of evil that had lodged themselves in the life and experience of oppressed individuals. Now these disciples were to be engaged in the same ministry. They were given authority to see people released from darkness and brought into the Kingdom of Light. Such release continues today. Jesus still sends his followers into the world to set captives free from evil in all its forms. Some will be dramatically decisive. Some will unfold over time, involving process, bringing healing.

Although Mark never recorded it for us, it's exactly what Jesus had announced back in the synagogue in Nazareth. *"The Spirit of the Lord is on me, because he has anointed me to preach good news to the poor. He has sent me to proclaim freedom for the prisoners . . . to release the oppressed . . ."* (Luke 4:18).

No wonder this was how he *"sent"* his disciples. No wonder it's our mission still.

Lord Jesus, I hear your call afresh in these verses. I receive the invitation to be with you. May I know you better and better, each day. I accept your commission. I engage in your mission. I choose to follow, closely, daily. Amen.

Reflect:

Is it easier for you to *"be with"* Jesus or to be *"sent"* by him? How can you step more firmly into both this day?

MARK 3:13-19 (PART 2)

These are the twelve he appointed: Simon (to whom he gave the name Peter); James son of Zebedee and his brother John (to whom he gave the name Boanerges, which means Sons of Thunder); Andrew, Philip, Bartholomew, Matthew, Thomas, James son of Alphaeus, Thaddaeus, Simon the Zealot and Judas Iscariot, who betrayed him.

(verses 16–19)

The first book of JRR Tolkien's beloved trilogy is titled *The Fellowship of the Ring*, introducing us to a mixed bag of characters on a quest through Middle Earth in opposition to the dark kingdom of Mordor. A mixed bag indeed! There's the wizard, Gandalf, who gives wise counsel and leadership. But then there's a dwarf and an elf, representatives of two races typically at loggerheads. There are four hobbits – halflings – whose small stature matches the minimal expectations everyone seems to have of them. Add to the mix two grown men, both warriors, one being the rightful, exiled King of Gondor, and the other being the son of the Steward who currently, jealously, guards the throne – they're set up for tension from the start.

I think Tolkien brilliantly captures the reality of human relationships generally, but specifically the reality of those who are called into mission for Jesus. We, too, are a pretty mixed bag.

Which is exactly what we see in this band of disciples Jesus appoints as apostles. The list puts Peter first and Judas Iscariot last. Judas fully deserves last place, for he betrays Jesus to death. Peter, on the other hand, seems to have rightfully earned first place, often emerging as leader of the fellowship. But, when push comes to shove, he denies even knowing Jesus when confronted at the fire in the High Priest's courtyard. Our list, then, is headed by one who disowns Jesus and concludes with one who betrays him. This is not a stellar group. Indeed, as Mark's Gospel unfolds, the disciples are portrayed in "surprisingly unfavourable light" (as one commentator rightly states[1]) – they are slow to understand who Jesus is, they bicker together, vie for position, succumb to fear, and ultimately abandon Jesus in his greatest moment of need in the Garden. Yet it's perversely encouraging, because if Jesus could use them, he can also use us. Indeed, he specifically chose each one, just as he has chosen each of us who follow. That we're all a mixed bag doesn't stop him.

The further thing to notice is how the group itself was set up for conflict right from the start. When Jesus invited the tax collector, Matthew Levi, to be one of his disciples, he brought into his inner circle one who was hated and despised by everyone in the surrounding area – including Peter, Andrew, James, John and Philip, who all lived there. Further, Matthew Levi was a collaborator with the hated Roman regime, which likely raised very intense issues for another of those chosen – Simon the Zealot. It's not entirely clear what "Zealot" implied at the time, but it likely meant his political perspective was intensely anti-Roman. He wouldn't warm naturally to a tax collector.

So, conflict was already simmering, if not boiling. Overlay on that the family relationships present in the group, with at least two sets of brothers, and possibly three or four. From time to time those brothers likely had their own squabbles. At other points (Mark

1   Larry Hurtado, *New International Biblical Commentary: Mark* (Peabody, MA: Hendrickson Publishers, 2001), 57-58.

10:35–37) they sided with each other against the rest. When you also realize that two of those brothers were nicknamed by Jesus "*Sons of Thunder*," you realize this was not a calm, peaceful mix.

And can't we identify with it all? We, too, are imperfect people. We, too, find ourselves in natural conflict and disagreement with some of those Jesus has chosen for our fellowship. Why should we be surprised? If it were up to us, we might simply bail. But he's the one who does the choosing. He's the one who brings us together. Can we trust him to use us, too, even as he used them? Can we press on alongside those we would never have chosen, but he did?

The Master has called. Will we follow?

Lord Jesus, thank you for calling me, choosing to use me, imperfect as I am. Thank you for choosing brothers and sisters around me – I receive them in the fellowship, even when I find them imperfect, too. Accomplish your purposes through us.

Reflect:
In Jesus, we are all on mission. In him, we are called into specific fellowship. Think of one (or more) in that grouping with whom you struggle. Speak to Jesus about them, committing yourself afresh to following his lead.

MARK 3:20-30

"I tell you the truth, all the sins and blasphemies of men will be forgiven them. But whoever blasphemes against the Holy Spirit will never be forgiven, he is guilty of an eternal sin."

(verses 28-29)

These verses sit there on the page, staring at me. I don't know what to do with them. I never have.

As I confront them afresh, struggling to understand, I am helped by a number of thoughts:

- I will keep on trusting the Lord – his wisdom, his goodness, his justice – even if I never come to a fully satisfactory understanding of this statement.

- Jesus' words come in a specific context. The religious leaders have claimed his work of casting out demons is truly the work of Satan, when actually it is nothing less than crystal clear evidence of the Spirit's activity among them (Matt 12:28).

- Such blinding disbelief keeps these teachers of the law from apprehending Jesus' true identity and, therefore, from placing faith in him.

- Lack of faith in Jesus, persisting for a lifetime, results in sin and guilt that remain intact; there is no other means of forgiveness.

All of this seems clear.

Yet questions remain:

- Have these teachers of the law, in making their statement (*"He is possessed by Beelzebub!"*), already committed the unforgivable sin? Is there no hope for them?

- On the other hand, if "persistent unbelief" is really the issue (as many of the commentators suggest), why is it categorized as blasphemy against the Holy Spirit, rather than blasphemy against the Son?

- Didn't Saul himself, with his committed Pharisaical perspective, come from such blind disbelief? Yet he travelled from spiritual darkness, through literal blindness, and then entered into saving faith in Jesus. Paul's situation was clearly redeemable, so the blasphemy Jesus speaks of here must somehow be different.

In the end, I am convinced that:

- Lack of faith in Jesus is a life and death issue.

- The Lord is gracious and just, wanting none to perish.

- He loves the world so very much he sent his Son to save us.

- There is no other name given among humanity by which we must be saved.

- I have believed. What grace.

Thank you, Lord Jesus. I entrust myself to you again. Thank you for saving me by your grace. Thank you that you reached out to me while I was still a sinner, still your enemy. Thank you that your love abounds.

Lord, you are fully trustworthy, fully just. Thank you I can trust even when I don't fully understand all of the issues. I see through a glass darkly, but you see clearly, with grace and compassion.

I entrust into your hands those I know and love who, as of yet, don't believe. Please bring them face to face with you. Please activate faith, that they might experience life. Like Saul, arrest them in their blindness, rescuing them into your Kingdom.

Praise the Name of Jesus. There is no other by which we must be saved.

Reflect:

Who has the Lord put on your heart for salvation? Pray for them, time and again, over this day. Pray they would have open eyes to see Jesus.

MARK 3:31-35

"Who are my mother and my brothers?" Jesus asked.

Then he looked at those seated in a circle around him and said, "Here are my mother and my brothers! Whoever does God's will is my brother and sister and mother."

(verses 33–35)

There seems to be conflict and tension between Jesus and his own natural family. They've come to *"take charge of him, for they said, 'He is out of his mind'"* (3:24). Ouch.

It helps us realize that even for those closest at hand in Jesus' earthly life, seeing wasn't necessarily believing. The intervention of God, coming in human flesh, was simply too much for most people to get their minds around all at once – the comprehension didn't come easily. Not even for mother and brothers. Wonderfully, though we're not told how, they eventually did come around. His mother, Mary, faithfully attended him at the foot of the cross as he died, then witnessed the resurrection, and was with the gathered disciples in the Upper Room prior to Pentecost. One of Jesus' brothers, James, ended up becoming a key leader in the early church in Jerusalem, writing a portion of the New Testament, as did another brother, Jude. Redemption comes.

But for the moment there is difficulty. Tension. Misunderstanding. Which is helpful for any who experience such family conflict in our own day. Jesus himself has been there. Indeed, he draws from his own experience later when he speaks of those who have *"left home or brothers or sisters or mother or father or children or fields for me and the gospel"* (Mark 10:29–30). Our Lord knows.

But there is another pressing encouragement in this passage for any who have chosen to follow Jesus. Here it is: He counts us family! We're part of his inner circle. We bear the same family name.

This is in line with the fact that we are called children of God. We have been adopted into the family of the Almighty, specially chosen, receiving the full rights of daughters and sons. We have a Father who loves us, calling us his own. Profound. Powerful. The Spirit himself bears witness with our spirit that this is true. We look to heaven and say from our hearts, *"Our Father."* And we find ourselves embraced.

And yet, what Jesus does here is different again. It takes the relationship from another angle, building intimate security on a different plane. For Jesus looks around the circle into our eyes, right at our level, side by side, one with us, and calls us family. He identifies himself with us, and us with him. As a brother, he welcomes us.

Oh, he is still Lord. Absolutely. For all eternity he commands our allegiance and reverence and worshipful adoration. Yet he stands upon the earth, looks in the eyes of those gathered round, and speaks the words, "Here is my family."

From the Gospel, these words echo now in my own ears, drawing me also into this familiarity of family relationship. My Lord is my brother. Praise his name.

———————

Lord Jesus, thank you. Your acceptance gives security. I choose to walk with you this day. Praise you.

———————

Reflect:
Take time to simply sit in the Lord's presence. Thank him for his love. Receive his acceptance afresh. Listen for his directions. Give him your day.

MARK 4:1-20

"Listen! A farmer went out to sow his seed. As he was scattering the seed, some fell along the path, and the birds came and ate it up. Some fell on rocky places, where it did not have much soil. It sprang up quickly because the soil was shallow. But when the sun came up, the plants were scorched, and they withered because they had no root. Other seed fell among thorns, which grew up and choked the plants, so that they did not bear grain. Still other seed fell on good soil. It came up, grew and produced a crop, multiplying thirty, sixty, or even a hundred times."

(verses 3–8)

"Still other seed fell on good soil."

Yes. Here's the farmer's motivation. This is what he's aiming at. Good seed in good soil that produces a good crop – indeed the potential is huge, the seed multiplying thirty or sixty or a hundred times over. It's incredibly worthwhile to be a farmer.

But failure looms large. Not every seed produces a crop. Indeed, there are more possible variations of failure than success: hard-packed path, rocky ground, thorny patches, yielding possibilities of seed falling prey to hungry birds, scorching sun, and nutrient-robbing weeds.

The farmer could focus on these hazards. If he did, he'd never scatter seed at all. The waste of seed and energy, hopes and dreams, would overwhelm him. If these disasters were front and centre in his mind, why would he bother? How foolish to expend such effort.

But clearly the farmer doesn't focus here. Oh, he knows it's a reality. He knows some of the seed released in each scattered handful will come to nothing. But his focus isn't there. It's on the rest of the seed, flying outward from his open hand, landing on that rich, moist soil before him, finding a home, rooting deeply, drawing nourishment, springing up. Good seed in good soil. That's what keeps him going.

In telling his story, Jesus reminds us of Kingdom realities. The incredible good news of salvation in Jesus will not always be matched by receptive hearts. Indeed, some will be outright hard and disinterested – maddeningly so. Others, seemingly enthusiastic, will respond with joy and delight, then hit bumps in the road, then waver and falter and let go of hope. Others, who at first are eagerly responsive, when it comes right down to it, will lose interest, grow distracted and move on.

Jesus is telling us not to be discouraged – this is the way of the world. But press on to fruitfulness. For when good seed meets good soil, the results can't be contained.

This is good news for preachers like me. There are so many times my own hopes are raised, only to be dashed. Yet seed is sown – there are eternal possibilities. And not only for preachers – this is good news for all who are part of Christ's Kingdom. All of us, in our way, are sent out as farmers, scattering seed through word and deed, hoping for harvest, but so often seeing the more immediate stony response, or withering interest, or blinding distraction. Good seed in good soil takes longer – at first merely hidden – is anything happening? But then growth becomes visible, and oh how good!

Don't hold the seed back. Let it fly.

Lord Jesus, strengthen my arm and determination to let seed fly. Give me endless hope, seeing through faith what can sprout and grow into eternity. Use me to see people step into life eternal. Amen.

Reflect:

Where can you cast seed this week? Ask the Lord if there is a person in your circle he is preparing to receive good seed.

MARK 4:21-25

He said to them, "Do you bring a lamp to put it under a bowl or a bed? Instead, don't you put it on its stand? For whatever is hidden is meant to be disclosed, and whatever is concealed is meant to be brought out into the open. If anyone has ears to hear, let him hear.

"Consider carefully what you hear," he continued. "With the measure you use, it will be measured to you - and even more. Whoever has will be given more, whoever does not have, even what he has will be taken from him."

"If anyone has ears to hear, let him hear."

I went for a hearing exam about a week ago. Some of my family had been telling me, for quite a while, that I should go, but I was having trouble hearing it (or at least listening!). I finally succumbed. I went into the little booth, put the headphones on, and pressed the buzzer every time I heard a sound. The upshot is that my hearing's not what it used to be - not quite as bad as it might be, thankfully, but clearly there are some frequencies I'm not hearing as well as one would expect.

I might need some extra help. I've got ears - but how well do they hear? That's the question.

At the end of the parable of the Sower and the Seed, which he's just told, Jesus spoke these words: *"He who has ears to hear, let him hear"* (4:9). Keeping spiritual ears keenly attuned is vital.

Indeed, it goes beyond hearing – the key issue is perceiving. Which is exactly what Jesus went on to say. Speaking to his disciples of *"the secret of the kingdom of God"* (4:11), he told them how some would be *"ever seeing but never perceiving, and ever hearing but never understanding"* (4:12). For those who were outside the circle of disciples, the sights and sounds of the Kingdom would remain just as hidden, just as secret, as ever. They wouldn't perceive. They wouldn't understand.

But Jesus intends otherwise. That's what he's telling us in this present passage. The good news of the Kingdom is meant to be seen. It's meant to be heard and perceived and understood. Although it's secret now – hidden and concealed – it's meant to be brought out into the open.

So, Jesus uses a powerful little illustration that apparently he used on a number of occasions in different ways. Matthew gives us one of those other instances (Matt. 5:14–16). It's the picture of a lighted lamp, brought into a room to give light. You don't put it under a bowl or stick it under the bed, do you? No! You put it on its stand so it can light up the house. When Jesus uses this mini-parable in Matthew's Gospel he's encouraging us to be light for the world, to let our good deeds shine before men so that they may give glory to God. The kids' song, "This Little Light of Mine," comes from that telling.

But Jesus uses the same picture here in a different way. He's telling us about the message of the Kingdom. Though hidden to so many – though secret and concealed – it's meant to be seen. Like a lamp on a stand, it's meant to shine out brightly.

And its sound is meant to clearly ring forth. *"If anyone has ears to hear, let him hear,"* Jesus says once more. Then he puts it out there again. *"Consider carefully what you hear,"* because if you have ears to hear the Kingdom message – if you receive it to heart and embrace it – you'll receive more. There will be more insight, more understanding, more of Jesus' message filling mind and heart. But, if your ears are closed, if your heart is hard, even what you think you've understood will wither away.

"If anyone has ears to hear, let him hear." It's the ongoing stance for life in Jesus. So, check your hearing.

———————

Lord Jesus, thank you for your ongoing message of the Kingdom. I submit my ears to hear. I submit my mind to ruminate. I submit my will to follow.

———————

Reflect:
Are you giving yourself time to hear? In what ways will you listen today?

MARK 4:26-29

He also said, "This is what the kingdom of God is like. A man scatters seed on the ground. Night and day, whether he sleeps or gets up, the seed sprouts and grows, though he does not know how. All by itself the soil produces grain – first the stalk, then the head, then the full kernel in the head. As soon as the grain is ripe, he puts the sickle to it, because the harvest has come."

I'm reminded of a bedtime story we used to read our kids. It was turned into a Claymation stop-action cartoon they loved to watch, called *Frog and Toad Together: The Garden.*

Toad admires Frog's garden and wants one, too. Frog gives him a bag of seed, but tells him having a garden is hard work. Undaunted, Toad heads off home to plant his seeds. Making a furrow in the soil, he carefully places each one in a nice, straight row, covering them with dirt, then stepping back to watch closely what will happen. Nothing does. Toad says, "Now seeds, start growing!" Still there's no response. More loudly he says, "Now seeds, start growing!" Still nothing. Impatiently, he shouts!

Right then, Frog arrives, telling Toad he's frightening the seeds. So, for the next several days, Toad works hard to calm his seeds, reading them bedtime stories, singing, reciting poetry, even playing his violin into the late-night hours. After many nights of these antics, he falls asleep on the ground, exhausted.

He's wakened in the morning by Frog, who points to the garden where sprouts are pushing their way up through the rich soil. Toad, ecstatic, says it was very hard work. Frog rolls his eyes.

The point, of course, in both stories, is that the gardener can't do anything to make the seed grow. Indeed, the farmer in Jesus' story, unlike any in real life, plants the seed and doesn't do a single thing more – no weeding or fertilizing or watering or tending of any kind. Yet the seed grows. All on its own. The farmer doesn't know how. The seed just grows.

The point that spills over from the previous parable (the Sower and the Seed) is that good seed in good soil gives amazing results. It's the same here. The point is that the fruitfulness of the Kingdom is irresistible.

It's not that we're to passively sit by, disengaging from Kingdom work. Not at all. There are plenty of other teachings in the New Testament encouraging us on into the joy of labouring in the Kingdom. But the point here is that the growth of Kingdom seed, planted in good soil, is absolutely inevitable. What huge encouragement to all of us farmers!

But there are two caveats. The first is that the process takes time. Night and day pass by. The farmer is sleeping and waking in succession, through many cycles. It takes time for the seed to germinate. Even then, when the sprout pushes its way up through the soil, the process of growth and maturation simply takes time. Harvest isn't immediate. Oh, how I need to remember this when I've put a heartfelt request before the Lord in prayer.

The second caveat is that for some of that time, the whole process is hidden. Is anything happening at all? We can't see. Again, this is the place I often find myself when I pray – so often, there's nothing whatsoever to see. I'm tempted to discouragement – is anything happening?

But the message of the parable is, "Yes, indeed!" When God's at work – when he's planted the seed – the result is inevitable. Irresistible.

Harvest is coming.

Thank you, Lord Jesus, for the sure hope of this simple story. Your work will come to full fruition. I trust you in the process. I watch for the harvest.

Pray:

What seeds of the Kingdom are keeping you waiting? Speak to the Lord about them. Grab hold of hope from this story afresh. Re-engage in faith-filled prayer.

MARK 4:30-34

*Again he said, "What shall we say the kingdom of God is like,
or what parable shall we use to describe it? It is like a mustard
seed, which is the smallest seed you plant in the ground.
Yet when planted, it grows and becomes the largest of all
garden plants, with such big branches that the birds
of the air can perch in its shade."*

(verses 30–32)

"Who despises the day of small things?" (Zech. 4:10).

This question was the Lord's way of encouraging Zerubbabel to
keep on rebuilding the Temple, which some critiqued as insignificant. So little. So small. Yet the power of God's Spirit would infuse
the work (*"Not by might nor by power, but by my Spirit,' says the
Lord Almighty"* Zech. 4:6).

If the foundations for the Temple could be viewed as inconsequential, how much more a tiny mustard seed? So little. So small.

"I thought the Kingdom of God would come with glory and
splash," we think. "Lord, where are you? Where is your handi-
work? How can this be what you have in mind?"

Yet, Jesus says, the Kingdom comes in often imperceptible
ways. We might almost completely miss its beginnings. We might
look right past. It might seem like no more than a dot in the palm
of our hand.

I think Jesus was speaking right into the reality of his own
ministry, in his own day. The common expectation was that the

Kingdom would come with huge smash – it would be a cataclysmic event, coming in wide-screen, technicolour, 3-D. They expected the Kingdom to be unmistakable, like a thunderbolt. They weren't expecting a mustard seed.

And though Jesus worked amazing miracles, for some the smash wasn't big enough. Even John the Baptist wondered. While in prison, he heard what Jesus was saying and doing, but nonetheless sent some disciples to ask, *"Are you the one who was to come, or should we actually expect someone else?"* I think he was saying: "Is this mustard seed all there is?"

Yet . . . that mustard seed is action-packed. So small, yet planted in the ground it holds unimaginable potential. Of course, once planted it will be even harder to see – indeed, completely hidden. But the future result will be massive, yielding a plant big enough, strong enough, with enough sturdy branches that even *"the birds of the air can perch in its shade."*

So, here's the big picture. The Kingdom will most certainly come in all its fullness. Jesus has promised to come again – he will. He will bring history to a conclusion, setting all to rights, fulfilling the prayer he himself taught, *"Your kingdom come, your will be done on earth as it is in heaven."* Perhaps you don't see anything at the moment. Perhaps what you do see isn't what you expected. It may seem small and insignificant, even inconsequential, like a mustard seed. But don't be fooled. Those small beginnings hold the guarantee of future fullness.

On the more immediate scale, there is also hope for our own prayer-filled yearnings. We entrust them into the Lord's hands, not always even knowing if our desires align with his. But as we pray according to his will, he hears us – and since we know he hears us, we know we have what we have asked of him. Even when we can't see it. Even when the beginnings seem, oh, so small. His Kingdom purposes will come to pass. They will grow and thrive and flourish. Have no doubt.

So, hang on to hope. Embrace faith. Mustard seeds yield huge growth.

_____

Lord Jesus, so many of the things I see at the moment are not yet in full Kingdom-proportions. Help me to rejoice whenever I see your activity, whatever its size and shape. Give me faith to press forward in prayer, anticipating your greater work. Amen.

_____

Pray:
Has some small beginning (or no visible beginning at all) dispirited your prayers? Take the mustard seed in hand and pray with renewed passion.

MARK 4:35-41

A furious squall came up, and the waves broke over the boat, so that it was nearly swamped. Jesus was in the stern, sleeping on a cushion. The disciples woke him and said to him, "Teacher, don't you care if we drown?"

He got up, rebuked the wind and said to the waves, "Quiet! Be Still!" Then the wind died down and it was completely calm.

(verses 37–39)

———

I had a horrible sleep last night, waking at about 3:00 am and lying, fitfully tossing, for over an hour and a half. It may have been induced by some late-night coffee, but it was mostly stress – stress over housing issues and finances that spilled over into church issues and relationships and a whole long list of things which need tending. Unsettled outward circumstances had invaded my soul.

How different is Jesus' experience. The wind is roaring, the waves are tossing, enough to unsettle veteran fishermen, yet Jesus is soundly asleep. Peace fills his soul, peace that is unruffled by the most raging storm.

And then, as if to demonstrate that inner calm, Jesus speaks it out into the world around him: *"Quiet! Be Still!"* With as much power as that first command – *"Let there be light!"* – Jesus' word once again creates a new reality. *"The wind died down and it was completely calm."* His peace reigns.

———

O Lord, the wind continues to whip around me this day. The fury threatens to make me as anxious as those disciples. Please, speak the divine word once again. "Quiet! Be still!"

I'll be still, yes, knowing that you are God. Whether the storm yet abates, may your presence, here with me in the midst, spread glassy calm within my soul.

I listen for your word, O my Lord.

Reflect:

What storm is churning the waters around you at the moment? Invite his voice to speak calm into your soul. Listen.

If the waters around you are currently calm, pray for someone else whose experience is storm-tossed. Pray for Jesus' peace.

MARK 5:1-20

Those tending the pigs ran off and reported this in the town and countryside, and the people went out to see what had happened. When they came to Jesus they saw the man who had been possessed by the legion of demons, sitting there, dressed and in his right mind; and they were afraid. Those who had seen it told the people what had happened to the demon-possessed man – and told about the pigs as well. Then the people began to plead with Jesus to leave their region.

(verses 14–17)

I've often thought of this passage as a New Testament horror story. It's got all of the creepy trappings of graveyard and wild-eyed lunacy and croaking demonic voices. But the real horror comes in geography.

The demons plead with Jesus *"not to send them out of the area"* (verse 10). And Jesus grants their request. He gives them permission to go into a nearby herd of pigs – so that's exactly what they do. You can imagine the demonic presence, that legion of sinister personalities, swarming the pigs, infesting their brains and bodies, terrorizing them through and through, resulting in them charging forward pell-mell, crashing into one another in blind terror, rushing off the cliff's edge to their death in the lake-water below. The pigs died. But the demons were still geographically present.

The pig herders rushed off to report the terror in the nearby town. Over time they had gotten fairly comfortable with the presence of the crazed demoniac living in the tombs. Often they'd tried to chain and bind him, but with super-human strength he'd broken all bonds, each and every time. They'd ended up striking a certain truce. They simply gave him a wide berth.

But this new development was different. Everyone gathered. They surveyed the scene: the hillside emptied of pigs, the carcasses floating near the shore, the desolate tombs, the broken chains. They took it all in, perceiving the dusty, lonely, sinister oppressiveness of it all. And in the midst, they saw the man sitting there, clothed, in his right mind, a smile on his face and intelligence in his eyes. And seeing him there, just like that, the crowd was terrified.

"Leave us alone," they pleaded with Jesus. "Hit the road. Give us a wide berth. Exit this region. Stay away."

So Jesus complies. In this is the horror. That swarming demonic contingent is still present. But Jesus, they've sent away. The story illustrates the tragic foolishness of human choices that push away the Lord.

Meanwhile, shalom has taken up residence in the life of this man who had previously been invaded by fractious discord. Filled with sanity and joy he passionately begs Jesus that he might travel with him, leaving that region far behind.

Ironically, his is the only request Jesus denies. For the sake of those who have chosen against him, Jesus sends the man back home to share with family everything God has done for him and to live out among them the mercy he himself has so abundantly received.

Darkness settled in that region. Human choices and spiritual forces of wickedness coalesced to put up barriers to the Kingdom. But the Lord planted one of his newly redeemed agents within that enemy territory to shine light into darkness.

In that is hope. Who knows? Did some of those folk later become members of the fledgling early church, tracing their own redemption back to the testimony of a raving lunatic who ended up clothed and in his right mind? Eternity will tell.

———————

Lord, give me eyes to see spiritual realities, ready to engage in your Kingdom work. I offer myself to you right here, in this very region you have placed me. Use me, O Lord.

———————

Reflect:

We, too, each live in enemy territory. Ask the Lord to use you today for his purpose. Then, watch for the opportunities. Bear witness in word and deed.

MARK 5:21-43

While Jesus was still speaking, some men came from the house of Jairus, the synagogue ruler. "Your daughter is dead," they said. "Why bother the teacher anymore?"

Ignoring what they said, Jesus told the synagogue ruler, "Don't be afraid; just believe."

(verses 35–36)

I remember back to Matthew's account of this event. He shortens the story considerably, presenting Jairus, from the very moment we meet him, as having death-confronting faith: *"My daughter has just died. But come and put your hand on her and she will live"* (Matt. 9:18).

Mark tells us how the man got to that place of faith. It's through the word of Jesus.

Jairus has faith enough to come in the first place to Jesus when his daughter is dying, steadily progressing to her grave. He's desperate. Desperation propels him. Falling at Jesus' feet, he pleads earnestly for the Master's healing touch.

But the announcement from home, *"Your daughter is dead,"* threatens to kill what faith he's got. This now slips into the realm of the impossible. Can faith survive?

Yes, it can, with the reviving impact of Jesus.

"Don't be afraid," he tells Jairus. This is one of the most familiar divine commands in scripture. Why? Because fear threatens to undo in our lives so much of what the Lord intends. Fear rises up

to tell Jairus that hope, now pointless, will only lead to inevitable disappointment. Protect yourself, fear says, and let go of faith. Jesus says otherwise. *"Don't be afraid; just believe."* What a powerful word in Jairus' ear right at that very moment. The words pronouncing his daughter's death are still ringing. Yet Jesus stills that echo, inviting ongoing faith. *"Just believe."* Jairus does. We know it from Matthew's record. *"My daughter has just died. But come and put your hand on her and she will live."* Wow.

Dear Lord Jesus, thank you that I am not alone in my faith. You are right here, cheering faith on, ready to speak the strengthening word when fear of disappointment rises up to quell what faith I have. Please make me sensitive to your voice, responsive to your word. "Just believe." Yes, Lord – I will.

Reflect:
What prayer are you praying at the moment that most needs this strengthening encouragement to *"just believe"*? Pray, and press forward like Jairus.

MARK 6:1-6

Jesus said to them, "Only in his hometown, among his relatives and in his own house is a prophet without honour." He could not do any miracle there, except lay his hands on a few sick people and heal them. And he was amazed at their lack of faith.
(verses 4–6)

Years back I prayed a prayer that launched me and our church, unexpectedly, into a grand adventure. *"Lord, enroll me in a practicum of faith."* The prayer was simple, straightforward, and heartfelt – it was what I really wanted.

The resulting practicum focused us in praying for individuals to come to faith through the people and ministries of our own congregation. Not a lot was happening in those days, so the stretch of faith was real. Week by week we prayed. Over the next year and a half, I journaled, filling the pages with the names of almost a hundred people who stepped into the Kingdom. We weren't a big church – the impact was huge.

This morning I feel that yearning again. *Lord, I need another practicum – please launch me afresh.*

This passage in Mark is filled with intense sadness. What loss. The Lord himself was in their very presence, ready to work. But they themselves weren't prepared. They were filled, rather, with un-faith, missing the moment.

Lord, I don't want to be in that category. Rescue me from the doldrums.

I find the word *"amazed"* riveting – and, oh, so sad. To cause amazement in the heart of God is a big thing. To cause it for the wrong reasons is a huge tragedy. I don't want to be in those shoes. I am reminded of another instance of Jesus' amazement. On that occasion Jesus was in his newly adopted hometown of Capernaum. He received a delegation from a Roman centurion whose highly valued servant was sick, on the brink of death. They pleaded with Jesus to come to his aid. As Jesus proceeded in response, the centurion sent other friends to hold him back, saying he didn't deserve Jesus to come under his roof, but that he could instead simply speak the word to heal the languishing servant, and all would be well. "I myself give orders to my subordinates," the centurion said, "and they act in response. I know about authority. So, just say the word – I know it will be enough."

Both Luke and Matthew, recording the incident, use the same word to describe Jesus' response: *"amazed"* (Matt. 8:10, Luke 7:9). Amazed at the man. Amazed at his faith. Amazed that such great faith had not yet been seen in all Israel.

I find myself standing in the balance. The possibility of amazement in the heart of my Lord is strong. May it not be the amazement provoked by Nazareth, causing him to be taken aback by faith's absence.

––––––––

Rather, Lord, stoke the fires of my faith that you may revel in the joy of amazement over faith that thrives. Though only mustard seed-sized, I will join you in amazed joy.

Launch me, Lord, in a practicum of faith.

––––––––

Reflect:

Will you pray the same prayer? Will you look for faith to grow? Will you step into the practicum, however the Lord leads?

MARK 6:6-13

They went out and preached that people should repent.
They drove out many demons and anointed many sick
people with oil and healed them.

(verses 12–13)

This chapter gives us a slice of life from Jesus' ministry, with miracles all over it. In his hometown of Nazareth, where Jesus is amazed at their lack of faith, Mark comments that *"he could not do any miracles there, except lay his hands on a few sick people and heal them"* (verse 5), which to me seems absolutely amazing for a low point!

The people grapple with who Jesus is because these *"miraculous powers are at work in him"* (verse 14). He feeds 5,000 with five loaves of bread and two fish. He walks on the surface of the lake as the disciples struggle to gain traction in a boat.

In the midst of this "slice" from Jesus' ongoing ministry, he confers authority on his disciples and they engage in miraculous ministry, too.

Again, I find myself stretched by the miracle-infused atmosphere of the Christian walk portrayed in the Gospels. I feel challenged by my own lack of expectation to see more.

Lord, rivet my heart with faith.

———————

In recent years, I have personally encountered a couple of stand-out moments of such Gospel-shaped faith. One came in an unexpected, out-of-the-way rural community in a church full of members who were themselves alive with expectancy, attentive to hearing and encountering God in tangible ways. Repentance and healing (of spirit, soul, and body), along with deliverance, were regular features of their life and ministry. Such expectation was infectious, inspiring many guests to look for the Lord's intervention in similar ways in their own church contexts.

Another sighting came in a weekend seminar hosted at a pair of churches in my own town, led by a teacher who was himself nurtured in Gospel-shaped faith. The teaching focused on issues of the deeper life, looking closely at the baggage of the soul, owning it, then repenting, breaking ties, seeking deliverance from evil's bondage, and connecting afresh with the Lord by his Spirit. Expectancy was present. The Lord was gracious. Blessing and breakthrough were the themes.

These personal encounters for me, along with many examples others could bring forward, give encouragement to lean more expectantly into the experience of the Gospels. The Lord Jesus commissioned his disciples to walk in his ministry. He commissions us, too.

But, as always, it's not about us. It's all about him. We watch and follow, expectant but not presumptuous.

———————

"I am trusting Thee, Lord Jesus, trusting only Thee."

O Lord Jesus, stretch me into faith that is infused with expectancy. May it be. Amen.

———————

Reflect:

Where do you need the transforming work of the Kingdom at work in your life right now? By faith, with expectancy, place it in Jesus' hands. Repeat the above prayer as the day progresses.

MARK 6:14-29

John had been saying to Herod, "It is unlawful for you to have
your brother's wife." So Herodias nursed a grudge against John
and wanted to kill him. But she was not able to, because Herod
feared John and protected him, knowing him to be a righteous
and holy man. When Herod heard John, he was greatly
puzzled, yet he liked to listen to him.

Finally the opportune time came.
(verses 18–21)

This is a tragic story. A key player in the unfolding story of salvation is cut down. The voice crying in the wilderness is silenced.

But it is also a cautionary tale about the insidiousness of temptation. The context is Herod's own life.

When Jesus was tempted by the devil in the wilderness over a period of forty days, he pushed the temptations aside, not succumbing to the enticement. That story ends with the notation that the devil *"left him until an opportune time"* (Luke 4:13). The evil one is always looking for opportunities.

As here with Herod. *"Finally the opportune time came."* Herodias' daughter, Salome (so named by Josephus in his historical writings), dances for Herod and his guests. Herod, pleased, makes rash promises. Asking her mother's counsel, Salome comes back with a horrific request: John's head on a platter. Herod, caught in the trap, does exactly what he had not wanted to do – he puts John to death. Poor Herod. Poor John.

Yet Herod had set himself up. This irony in the story is high-lighted when we're told *"Herod feared John and protected him, knowing him to be a righteous and holy man"* (verse 20). One wants to ask: "Then why, O Herod, did you not release John from prison?" That would have been the ultimate protection. It would have been the ultimate affirmation of his righteous and holy status.

But, no, Herod kept John imprisoned because John had spoken out against his unlawful relationship with Herodias. He held him under threat of execution, fully intending never to exercise it. Yet, perhaps without thinking, he hung on to the option.

Doesn't that sound like a typical case of flirting with tempta-tion? Like the person who is intent on consuming less calories, but stocks their pantry with all sorts of calorie-rich treats. Or the guy intent on overcoming pornography, who nonetheless surfs the web unhindered, skirting the edge of what's risqué. Or the one who has foresworn gossip, but engages in regular, prolonged conversation with those who haven't.

So Herod found himself backed into a corner. Oh yes, his arro-gance and pride were fully involved. Boastfully, he'd made a brazen promise to impress his guests. Pridefully, he wouldn't back down when Herodias and Salome schemed to push the limits. But he'd already set himself up by keeping John imprisoned. The tragedy of a head on a platter had always been a possibility.

Herod's story remains a cautionary tale. *"Flee the evil desires of youth,"* Paul tells his young friend, Timothy (2 Tim. 2:22). It's good advice at any age and stage. Don't keep options for sin locked up in reserve. Empty the dungeon.

Lord Jesus, show me any options I'm keeping open when it comes to sin and temptation. Even as I pray "lead me not into temptation,"

*strengthen me to choose paths that align with you. Teach me to resist
the devil. Teach me to resist sin. To your glory. Amen.*

———————

Reflect:

As you've prayed, is there anything the Lord has shown you that
needs to be emptied out to avoid future temptation? What steps do
you need to take?

MARK 6:30-44

Because so many people were coming and going that they didn't even have a chance to eat, he said to them, "Come with me by yourselves to a quiet place and get some rest."

So they went away by themselves in a boat to a solitary place. But many who saw them leaving recognized them and ran on foot from all the towns and got there ahead of them. When Jesus landed and saw a large crowd, he had compassion on them, because they were like sheep without a shepherd. So he began teaching them many things.

(verses 31–34)

This passage gives us a full sighting of the compassionate sensitivity of Jesus – indeed, twice over. The apostles return from their mission trip, giving the Master a complete report of their words and deeds. Jesus knows they need rest. He knows the current context, with crowds everywhere, won't allow it. So, he takes them away by boat to a solitary place. He feels for them.

But the scenario takes on a new dimension as a massive crowd of eager followers, running ahead, converge on the very spot that Jesus and his disciples are heading. Jesus sees the crowd and understands their need. Mark tells us that *"he had compassion on them, because they were like sheep without a shepherd"* (verse 34), using a metaphor that is used at several points in the Old Testament to speak of the precarious position of God's people when they find

80

themselves leaderless and cast adrift. That's how Jesus perceives this eager crowd on the shore of Galilee. And he feels for them.

Matthew employs the very same phrase (*"sheep without a shepherd"*) at a different point in his narrative, using it as part of a summary statement of Jesus' ongoing ministry of teaching and miracle-working (Matt. 9:36). I take it as a general description of his motivation for ministry. Indeed, it is why he came – to seek and to save those who were lost.

But the word that stands out to me once again in this passage comes before the metaphor of sheep and shepherd. It's the gutsy word *"compassion."* We've encountered it before. It's that graphic word that finds its root in the Greek word for "bowels." This is deep-seated compassion that resonates from Jesus' very core, welling up in heartfelt motivation to bless the people. The Greek word itself is *splanchnizomai* – it's got a memorable, guttural ring.

No wonder Jesus interrupts his immediate plans. No wonder he chooses not to follow the disciples' advice to hurriedly send the crowd away unfed. No wonder he works a miracle instead that all four of the Gospel writers record for us. No wonder he meets the crowd's immediate need so they could linger longer to hear more of his teaching, meeting eternal needs.

It's because of *splanchnizomai*. He has gut-level compassion for the people. It's indicative of his whole ministry. Still. It's his orientation toward us.

And so I am not surprised when I discover Paul using the same root word in Philippians 1:8 as he speaks of *"the affection of Christ Jesus."* Can't you see it? Can't you sense it? The very heart of Jesus himself feels deeply for you. He pays attention. He sees your need. He works on your behalf, for your good, for your eternal blessing.

So, as I read this story, repeated four times over in the Gospels, I understand that it is not only a true recounting of history. It's certainly that – but it's more.

"Compassion" is an expression of Jesus' heart for me.

Thank you, Lord Jesus, for your affection, your deep-seated love, your compassion. I see it here in your hands as they break bread for thousands seated on the green grass. I see it more clearly yet in your hands, winning salvation, nailed to that bloodied cross. Your love has motivated your sacrificial gift. Praise you. I receive.

Reflect:
Take the phrase *"the affection of Christ Jesus"* and live with it all day. Call it to mind often. Ponder its depths. Express your thanks. Receive his compassion.

MARK 6:45-56

He saw the disciples straining at the oars, because the wind was against them. About the fourth watch of the night he went out to them, walking on the lake. He was about to pass by them, but when they saw him walking on the lake, they thought he was a ghost. They cried out, because they all saw him and were terrified.

Immediately he spoke to them and said, "Take courage! It is I. Don't be afraid." Then he climbed into the boat with them, and the wind died down.

(verses 48–51)

This is the second of two "sea miracles" in Mark's Gospel. The first (4:35–41) was the tempestuous storm on Galilee, severe enough to unsettle even veteran fishermen. Meanwhile, Jesus himself was asleep in the back of the boat. That chaotic experience shot terror through all those storm-tossed disciples.

This scene is different. Fear isn't the initial issue. Rather, it's hard work. It seems they are rowing and rowing, with very little headway. Indeed, when Mark describes the disciples *"straining at the oars,"* the word he uses implies it was "tortuous."

The resolution in the first instance came when Jesus spoke his own peace into the disciples' chaotic environment. *"Peace – be still."* He spoke it, and it was.

The resolution in the second instance is more convoluted. Ultimately, it's Jesus' abiding presence with them in the boat, punctuated by the revelatory phrase, *"I am,"* that makes the difference. But the disciples pass through intense fear before getting there.

The incident starts with Mark giving us an insight beyond either of the other Gospels that record this event. *"He saw the disciples straining at the oars"* – that's what Mark tells us. This is the powerful motive force for the whole encounter. The compassion Jesus had earlier felt for his disciples in taking them away to a quiet place apart, and then the compassion he felt for the masses who were like sheep without a shepherd, is now the same compassion rising up within him as he sees the disciples labouring unfruitfully against a force-filled headwind. So *"he went out to them."* His intent is clear. He cares for the disciples in their struggle. He chooses to make a difference.

We're surprised, then, when Mark tells us *"he was about to pass by them."* How can that be? It's possible that Mark gives us the uninformed perspective of the disciples in the boat – for all they could tell, filled with fear as they were, the apparition on the water was simply passing by.

But there is another possibility that rings true with Jesus' intention. Mark may intentionally be using a figure of speech from the Old Testament to describe a sighting of Almighty God. Such a theophany takes place when Moses pleads with God to show him his glory. The Lord tells him, *"I will cause all my goodness to pass in front of you"* (Ex. 33:19). And that's what happens. *"He passed in front of Moses"* (Ex. 34:6), proclaiming his name, bestowing a revelation of himself.

That's what Jesus does here. He makes himself known. He treads the waves, like Almighty God in the Old Testament (Job 9:8). He speaks the divine name – *"I am"* (that's the literal translation of *"It is I!"*). In the midst of the storm, in the midst of their anguished struggle, Jesus makes himself known.

Then he climbs into the boat. The wind dies down. All is well.

Open my eyes, O Lord. I, too, want to see you, to know you afresh. Thank you that this is your desire – to make yourself known. In the midst of the storm, in the midst of my labours, you come alongside. I welcome you, today.

Receive:

The Lord has promised he will never leave us nor forsake us. He is with us by his Spirit. Take time to welcome him now. Remind yourself regularly as you walk with him today.

MARK 7:1-23

He went on: "What comes out of a man is what makes him unclean. For from within, out of men's hearts, come evil thoughts, sexual immorality, theft, murder, adultery, greed, malice, deceit, lewdness, envy, slander, arrogance and folly. All these evils come from inside and make a man unclean."

(verses 20–23)

The Pharisees and teachers of the law understood the concept of clean versus unclean completely. They had it nailed. If they had lived in a COVID-world, as we have, they would have been the poster boys of handwashing! Not that they did it extremely vigorously, but they did it with full-throttled fastidiousness. They would cup their hands in a certain way, pouring water over the extended fingers and allowing it to rinse every part of the hand. They did it regularly, washing hands before morning prayer, before each meal, and certainly any time they came in from the marketplace.

In so doing they took the Old Testament handwashing regulations for priests and extended them to everyone – at least everyone who wanted to be "holy." As a result, they assumed a person's rigid adherence to the rules indicated spiritual commitment and that any neglect showed gross indifference. For them, *"cleanliness is next to godliness"* was too weak a statement. Rather, they believed the two were identical.

Jesus cuts through it all. Not that handwashing is a bad thing. It just doesn't have any bearing on holiness. *"These people honour me with their lips,"* he quotes Isaiah as saying, *"but their hearts are far from me"* (7:7).

It's an important statement, because it turns out the heart, rather than the hands, is the key location for cleanliness. That's where all manner of uncleanness originates, Jesus says: *"evil thoughts, sexual immorality, theft, murder, adultery, greed, malice, deceit, lewdness, envy, slander, arrogance and folly."* It's an oppressive line-up, and it's helpful to know that good hand hygiene, while useful, doesn't deal with any of it. Holiness is a heart issue that spills forth into the whole of life.

Practically it means the scruples of the Pharisees and teachers of the law don't need to hobble Jesus' disciples. But it does point out a much bigger issue. If it's a matter of the heart, how do we ensure we're clean?

Already, Jesus' teaching is pointing to the fact we need divine rescue. Already, we're being prepared for the cleansing sacrifice of the cross. Oh, how we need it. This awareness paves the way for the Apostle Paul's later insight that we can only put off the old self (*"which is being corrupted by its deceitful desires"*) and put on the new self (*"created to be like God in true righteousness and holiness"*) by being made new in the attitude of our minds (Eph. 4:22–24), a work that is accomplished solely by Christ through the Spirit.

But that understanding awaits the cross. At this point in Mark's Gospel, we're simply reminded of the leprous man, desperately crying out to Jesus, *"If you are willing, you can make me clean"* (Mark 1:40). He knew he had no other possibility.

So, too, for us, with uncleanness of every kind welling up within. We need a Healer. We need a Saviour. We, too, cry out.

And we hear the strong, compassionate reply, *"I am willing. Be clean!"* (Mark 1:41).

Hand hygiene may result from ritual scrubbing. But our desperate hearts need Jesus.

———————

Lord Jesus, thank you that you have seen my need. Thank you for providing the full cleansing I require. Help me to put off the old, be renewed by your Spirit in my mind, and put on the new, the fresh, the clean. Thank you – it's all from you.

———————

Receive:

The Spirit wants to renew your mind, all day. Cooperate. Create room by putting off the old (behaviours and attitudes not pleasing to Jesus). Submit to the Spirit's renewal. Live it out by putting on the new (all that Jesus calls you to do). Live clean.

MARK 7:24-30

The woman was a Greek, born in Syrian Phoenicia. She begged Jesus to drive the demon out of her daughter.
(verse 24)

This is a fascinating story – troubling from some perspectives. Jesus seems to initially brush the woman off. In Matthew's account, he doesn't even answer her at first, despite her persistent pleadings. The disciples eventually intervene, urging him to send her away, eliciting his response: *"I was sent only to the lost sheep of Israel"* (Matt. 15:24).

Mark skips past all of that, but emphasizes, more strongly than Matthew, the woman's outsider pedigree. She's not part of Israel, not inside the circle of God's people. That's what catches my eye this morning – we'll come back to it.

But first, just a reflection on what's going on here. I think Jesus spots faith in this woman right from the start and then temporarily pushes back on her request in order to allow that faith to show its strength, indeed to flex and grow. She rises to the challenge, pressing forward with bold persistence. Jesus grants her request, affirming that she has *"great faith"* (Matt. 15:28). I imagine the woman and her daughter were eternally shaped by this brief encounter. Eternity will tell.

But back to her pedigree. She couldn't be more clearly outside the circle. She was a non-Jew, living outside Israel, with no claim to any birthright other than Gentile. By those criteria, she would be considered "unclean," indeed as unclean as the disciples' unwashed hands that deeply troubled the Pharisees (Mark 7:5). They focused completely on external markers, like physical hands and place of birth and ethnic background. But Jesus emphasized a far deeper criteria for "clean-ness" other than simply hands which had been ritually sanitized. No, he said, the issue has to do with what's inside a person, what's in their heart. That's the place that uncleanness festers. That's the location needing cleansing. The state of external hands doesn't really have a bearing.

So, too, with external birthright. This woman had the wrong pedigree, yet Jesus grants her request. He does it while emphasizing his abiding commitment to the people of Israel. Indeed, they have priority in his current ministry – *"First let the children eat all they want,"* he says (verse 27). But clearly, he doesn't see this woman as irredeemably "unclean" – not at all. Instead, he stretches her faith, exposing its strength, and then brings her under the blessing of his care. It's a picture of salvation. It's a picture of welcoming embrace.

By the time Mark wrote his Gospel, the early church was filled with a wonderfully diverse mix of humanity, Gentiles equally with Jews, a community in which *"there is neither Jew nor Gentile, neither slave nor free, nor is there male and female, for . . . all (are) one in Christ Jesus"* (Gal. 3:28).

Imagine the scene, then, at one of those early gatherings of worship, as those who could not trace their heritage to Israel came upon this story in Mark's Gospel. Imagine the sense of familiarity and belonging as they heard the scripture and, in their mind's eye, saw Jesus encountering this woman outside the circle, a woman who simply by her ethnicity was considered "unclean." Imagine their joy as Jesus affirmed her faith, granted her request, and allowed her to taste the presence of the Kingdom.

Imagine the thankfulness of renewed realization that this story was theirs, too.

———————

Thank you, Lord Jesus, that though outside the circle, without any right of entry, you have welcomed me into your Kingdom. It's all of your grace. Praise your name.

———————

Reflect:
The woman had no right to expect Jesus' answer to her request. And yet she received it. It's called grace. Reflect on some of the many gifts of undeserved grace you yourself have received. Give thanks.

MARK 7:31-37

After he took him aside, away from the crowd, Jesus put his fingers into the man's ears. Then he spit and touched the man's tongue. He looked up to heaven and with a deep sigh said to him, "Ephphatha!" (which means, "Be opened!"). At this, the man's ears were opened, his tongue was loosened and he began to speak plainly.

(verses 33–35)

"*Be opened!*" This is a prayer I take to myself this morning.

I have been praying a messianic prophecy for myself, really for years, but renewed over the last week. Not with delusions of grandeur. Rather, knowing I am "*in Christ,*" I pray that what was true of Jesus might increasingly be true of me.

> "*The Sovereign Lord has given me an instructed tongue,*
> *to know the word that sustains the weary.*
> *He wakens me morning by morning,*
> *wakens my ear to listen like one being taught.*
> *The Sovereign Lord has opened my ears,*
> *and I have not been rebellious,*
> *I have not drawn back.*" (Isa. 50:4–5)

Now I hear this liberating Aramaic command, "*Ephphatha!*" And I pray:

"*Do it, Lord.*" *Open my ears – waken them to your voice. Thank you for the hearing you have bestowed. But so often it is dull, distracted, clouded, clogged. Unstop my ears. Put your fingers in and clear them out. Speak "Ephphatha!" over me, clearing each one. Touch my tongue. May it be instructed, equipped to sustain those who need sustenance, who have been wearied. Take this deaf mute, O Lord, and make me more like you.*

Amen.

Pray:

Invite the Lord's ear-opening work in your own experience today. Ask him to speak in ways that you can hear. Then set your heart to listen.

MARK 8:1-13

During those days another large crowd gathered. Since they had nothing to eat, Jesus called his disciples to him and said, "I have compassion for these people; they have already been with me three days and have nothing to eat . . .".

His disciples answered, "But where in this remote place can anyone get enough bread to feed them?"

"How many loaves do you have?" Jesus asked.
(verses 1–5)

At what point in this encounter do you think the sense of déjà vu became overwhelming for the disciples? Just two chapters earlier they'd experienced the feeding of the five thousand, punctuated by twelve basketfuls of leftovers (one for each pair of hands) and the riveting sight of Jesus walking on the surface of the water. Pretty unforgettable stuff.

Yet, maybe not. Here they are again with a need that seems overwhelmingly impossible. Four thousand people, three days' worth of hunger, and the only food in sight being a handful of loaves and a few small fish.

(Loaves and fish, did you say? Hmm, that reminds me of something.)

One wonders that they didn't choke on their words as they voiced their query, *"Where in this remote place can anyone get enough bread to feed them?"* As if they were saying, *"Who's ever heard of such a thing?"*

We, of course, get the advantage of Mark's story-telling. He condenses the events so we clearly see the highlights. Who knows how may incidents had transpired since that last great feeding. But for us, it was only two chapters ago. And then, lest we're caught off guard, he alerts us afresh right off the top, by telling us that *"another large crowd gathered."* This looks familiar, we think.

Yet I'm struck by the fact that in my own narrative I often miss the markers. How many times has the Lord worked in my life to meet me in my need, and yet I face the next challenge with the same overwhelmed query: *"Where in this remote place can anyone get enough?"*

O Lord, forgive me for the times I have forgotten so quickly. I have received from your hand grace upon grace, yet I can be anxious and confused when that next season of hungry need presents itself.

Strengthen faith within me by awakening remembrance. May I see your hands, know your face, trust your power, and yield to your compassion. Again.

Reflect:
Take some time to think back over the past twelve months. What markers of the Lord's intervention have you seen? Call them to mind. Dust them off. Write them down. Give thanks afresh. And ask the Lord to prepare you with faith for the next need.

MARK 8:14-21

Aware of their discussion, Jesus asked them: "Why are you talking about having no bread? Do you still not see or understand? Are your hearts hardened? Do you have eyes but fail to see, and ears but fail to hear? And don't you remember? When I broke the five loaves for the five thousand, how many basketfuls of pieces did you pick up?"

"Twelve," they replied.

"And when I broke the seven loaves for the four thousand, how many basketfuls of pieces did you pick up?"

They answered, "Seven."

He said to them, "Do you still not understand?"
(verses 1–5)

Once again the disciples are in a boat with Jesus on Galilee. Once again they have just experienced the miraculous multiplication of bread and fish to feed a massive crowd. Once again their own supply of bread is not adequate for their need. They've got but one loaf between them. They'd forgotten to bring more. Whatever happened to the seven basketfuls they'd just collected?

In their negligence they are immediately struck with guilt when Jesus mentions yeast, and they become distracted from what he's really trying to tell them.

How often does this happen for me, Lord? My own guilt gets in the way. Or false-guilt from an overly sensitive conscience rises up regarding issues that don't really matter. Or prideful thinking envelopes me, causing me to think everything depends on me.

Jesus cuts through all the immediate issues and gets to the main point. The disciples need to have a reset in terms of their perspective on life. Jesus is able. That's the point. When they'd previously found themselves in situations of impossible need – confronting five thousand hungry men, plus women and children, or again some four thousand – Jesus was able. The little they'd had was no impediment to the abundance of the Master. So, why were they fretting now when need confronted them again, even when brought on by their own negligence?

They needed to fully embrace what the Lord had shown them. They needed eyes to see and ears to hear and soft hearts to receive it all, altering their default outlook.

When he'd shared with them the Parable of the Sower and the Seed, he'd told them they were entrusted with the secret of the Kingdom, while those outside would be *"ever seeing but never perceiving, and ever hearing but never understanding"* (Mark 4:12). Now, in the boat, he rebukes them for their own dullness.

I, too, am journeying with Jesus. For me, also, the outlook is transformed. Do I see it? Do I hear? Is my heart receptive? The hands of my Lord are capable enough to provide for me in the midst of every need, even those of my own making. *"His divine power has given us everything we need for life and godliness"* (2 Peter 1:3).

I lift my sights from that meager single loaf to gaze instead on his ample provision in all things.

Lord Jesus, please increase faith within me today, trusting that you are able, that your provision will be enough. Keep me from being distracted by focusing on myself – my own insufficiency, neglect, meager offering. Instead, lift my sights fully and clearly to you. Focus my attention. Clear the blurred vision.

———————

Reflect:

What need are you feeling most keenly today? What resource do you have to meet it? Measure the gap, and give it into Jesus' hands. Remind yourself often: *His divine power has given us everything we need.*

MARK 8:22-26

They came to Bethsaida, and some people brought a blind man and begged Jesus to touch him. He took the blind man by the hand and led him outside the village. When he had spit on the man's eyes and put his hands on him, Jesus asked, "Do you see anything?"

He looked up and said, "I see people; they look like trees walking around."

Once more Jesus put his hands on the man's eyes. Then his eyes were opened, his sight was restored, and he saw everything clearly.
(verses 22–25)

———————

"Do you have eyes but fail to see?" (Mark 8:18). Jesus' pointed question to his disciples in the boat has just been recounted for us by Mark. There's no mistake. He wants us to check our sight also.

There are so many details in this short encounter that stand out. The care and compassion of the people for their blind neighbour. Their utter faith that Jesus' touch will bring healing. The tenderness of Jesus taking the man by the hand to lead him. The prophetic fulfilment implicit in that simple act — *"I will lead the blind by ways they have not known"* (Isa. 42:16). The fact that Jesus takes him out of the mainstream, to a quieter place outside town. And then there's the spit – tangible, graphic, messy, intimate.

But the greatest intrigue comes with the gradual progression of the healing. Why? What was happening? Why was this miracle a two-stager, when Jesus' healings are most often simple, straightforward, direct in their full effectiveness?

We don't know what was being accomplished for the man himself through this protracted healing. Perhaps his soul needed that extra time and attention in order to fully engage with new health.

But beyond the man himself, this miracle is an acted parable. The disciples have been entrusted with the very secrets of the Kingdom (Mark 4:11), their spiritual eyes opened to revelation from Jesus himself. Even so, they were not yet seeing clearly. Their perception was clouded, their spiritual focus blurred. The Healer, Jesus himself, was touching their lives, and yet the work was not complete – focus needed to be sharpened.

I remember back in elementary school when the teacher would set up one of those ancient projectors to show us a filmstrip. She'd be at the front of the class, having engaged one privileged student to man the projector at the back of the room. The blurred image would come on the screen, and she'd say, *"Sharpen it. Sharpen it. Sharpen it."* And with each command the image would tighten, get crisper, finally resolving into clear focus.

That's what happens for the blindman. It's what Jesus desires for the disciples.

It's what I need.

Eyes on Jesus, focused clear.

Dear Lord Jesus, please sharpen the focus. Touch my eyes this day to see you clearly. There are so many things which cloud my vision. I confess to you the ones I know. I entrust to you the ones I don't. Clear them all away. Burn away the fog. Let me see you, only.

Reflect:

What events and concerns and distractions threaten to cloud your vision today. Entrust them into Jesus' hands. Ask him to sharpen the focus now. Check in with him during the day, regularly, to sharpen it again.

MARK 8:27-30

"But what about you?" he asked. "Who do you say I am?"

Peter answered, "You are the Christ."
(verse 29)

———————

Finally! In the very first verse of his Gospel, Mark has clearly given us Jesus' full identity, naming him as Christ and Son of God. Since then we've heard the Father from heaven declare Jesus to be his Son. We've heard demons calling out that he is Son of God. But so far no human voice has declared his true identity.

Until now.

The disciples, ever since their calling, have been given a front row seat. They've had access to the secret of the Kingdom. They've watched Jesus' divine acts of power, overcoming the demonic and sickness and forces of nature and even death. Yet along the way, from these prime seats, we've heard them puzzling over his identity. *"Who is this? Even the wind and the waves obey him!"* (4:41).

Until now. On this occasion, Peter nails it. *"You are the Christ."* Finally. The disciples, having been given eyes to see, are now seeing.

It strikes me that Mark has very carefully crafted his narrative. He's just told us the story of the progressive healing of the blind-man at Bethsaida, a story which none of the other Gospel writers record. At first, the man had only seen through a blur, perceiving people *"like trees walking around"* (8:24). But Jesus touches him again, and "bingo" – his sight comes clear.

That's Peter's experience here. The image sharpens. Jesus comes into focus. Peter sees clearly. In Matthew's Gospel, Jesus immediately tells Peter *"this was not revealed to you by man, but by my Father in heaven"* (Matt. 16:17). In Mark's account, Jesus' healing of the blindman immediately prior serves the same purpose. For clear sight, you need the divine touch.

As the rest of the Gospel unfolds, it's clear that Peter and the disciples don't fully retain this clarity. There will be much doubt and confusion yet, including the blind desertion of the Master in his moment of greatest need. The abiding clarity of vision awaits the cross and resurrection and out-pouring of the Spirit. Even then, human frailty requires the ongoing refreshing of sight, being sharpened by worship, nourished by bread and wine, and refocused by the truth-sharpening presence of the Spirit.

"Open the eyes of my heart, Lord. Open the eyes of my heart. I want to see you. I want to see you."

It's our ongoing need. It should be our ongoing prayer.

So, Lord Jesus, touch my eyes as you did the blindman. Father, grant revelation to my mind as you did Peter's. Holy Spirit, lead me into truth, as you love to do – bring glory to Jesus, the Christ, the Son of the Living God. Amen.

Action:

Take Peter's simple statement, *"You are the Christ,"* and speak it back to Jesus again and again throughout the day. In moments of decision, crisis, conversation, leisure, care-giving, speak this declaration. Then seek to live it.

MARK 8:31–9:1 (PART 1)

He then began to teach them that the Son of Man must suffer many things and be rejected by the elders, chief priests and teachers of the law, and that he must be killed and after three days rise again. He spoke plainly about this, and Peter took him aside and began to rebuke him.

(verses 31–32)

At a surprisingly early point in the story we discovered that the religious leaders were plotting to kill Jesus (3:6). Now, for the first time, we hear Jesus himself speaking plainly and matter-of-factly about his impending execution. He doesn't raise alarms about it being a conspiracy. He doesn't seem cowed or threatened – not at all. He doesn't complain about its injustice. No. He simply explains that it's going to happen.

He will suffer many things, he says, and be rejected by the faith leaders of the nation, and then be killed. After three days, he said, he would rise.

Shortly, we will discover Peter and James and John discussing with one another *"what 'rising from the dead' meant"* (9:10). So, though Jesus spoke plainly, some of what he said was simply too far out of the box to be apprehended. But Peter certainly caught the part about death. He caught it, and he didn't like it. So he rebuked Jesus. Told him off. He let Jesus know that couldn't happen. Never.

It becomes clear why Jesus, all the way along, has stifled any talk of him being "Son of God" or "Christ." The statements are entirely true, as Mark has told us in the very first verse of his Gospel, but prior to the cross they could only lead to misunderstanding of his purpose and mission. Here we have the proof. Peter had as clear a view as anyone into Jesus' person and ministry. He'd heard teaching and insights beyond most. He'd seen miracles and wonders right up close, in the front row. Yet the idea of Jesus willingly submitting to suffering, rejection, and execution are simply beyond him. They offend him to the core. These are not the things that should happen to the Lord's anointed. At least, so he thought.

We, however, know the end of the story. It doesn't come as a surprise. But what is reinforced for us is that Jesus was intentionally heading to the cross all along. This is what it means for him to be "Christ."

In one of Isaiah's Servant Songs we hear the Lord's Servant (Messiah – Jesus himself) speaking these words:

"The Sovereign Lord has opened my ears,
and I have not been rebellious;
I have not drawn back.
I offered my back to those who beat me,
my cheeks to those who pulled out my beard;
I did not hide my face
from mocking and spitting . . .

I set my face like flint . . ." (Isa. 50:5–7)

That's what we see here. Jesus knew why he'd come. He knew exactly where he was going. He set his face like flint, not hanging back, not veering aside, instead pressing forward, step by obedient step, closing in on his goal, the task of giving *"his life as a ransom for many"* (Mark 10:45).

What focus. What determination.

Hallelujah! What a Saviour!

Praise you, Lord Jesus, that you came to seek and to save the lost, knowing full well it would cost you everything. Praise you, that you never flinched, but stayed obedient to the Father, keeping your eyes on the goal. Praise you, that you expressed the full extent of your love for me, for all, by laying down your life, the Good Shepherd for the sheep. Praise you.

Reflect:
Pause to reflect on the Lord's determination. The crucifixion was horrific – yet he'd known all along it was his destination. Understand that your own salvation – specifically, lovingly – was part of that plan all along, since the very creation of the world. Sit back. Wonder. Give thanks.

MARK 8:31–9:1 (PART 2)

"If anyone would come after me, he must deny himself and take up his cross and follow me. For whoever wants to save his life will lose it, but whoever loses his life for me and for the gospel will save it."
(verses 34–35)

———————

Lord, these words are central to the Gospel. They flow directly out of your own commitment to the sacrifice of the cross. They imply the necessity of identifying fully with you, embracing the same attitude that you yourself embraced, laying aside my own rights and desires and goals, and taking up yours.

These words have been with me all my life. Yet, oh, how they stretch and challenge, still. Oh, how they trouble me with questions: "Have I taken up my cross? Am I truly carrying it now?"

So what does it mean for me, right now, to deny myself and take my cross and follow? So much of my life is established, running on set tracks, constrained by previous decisions and experiences and commitments. So much, I confess, is comfortable.

Lord, what do you say in the midst of this? What do you want from me?

I hear you say, "All."

I hear you say, "Follow me in each moment, in each circumstance. Don't wait to recreate the landscape. Follow, starting right where you are."

———————

So often I focus on the heroics of those who have launched into grand adventures, expansive endeavours, vast visions. It may be that my Lord will choose to use me in some unexpected way, shifting my context, or sending me away into a new environment. But the place he calls me to carry my cross right now is right here. It's in the midst of family and church and neighbourhood and established relationships and conflicts and conundrums and queries. This is the present landscape. This is the launching pad. This is the place. At least for now.

So, soul, take up the cross. Your attitude should be the same as that of the Lord. Humbly serve. Consider others better than yourself. Wash feet. Lay aside rights. Seek to save the lost. Bind up wounds. Give to the poor. Pray as if mountains can be moved. Employ mustard seed-sized faith, watching for Jesus to act. Do it, here and now.

Engage with the Lord.

———————

Lord Jesus, I hear your command. I choose to follow. I confess that along the way I will not always know what "following" actually means. I confess that when I "know," I may have difficulty doing it. But it is my intent to follow. Please strengthen me by your Spirit to do so.

———————

Pray:
Reflect on the above prayer. What will it mean for you? Shape it with your own words. Pray it. Listen. Follow.

MARK 9:2-13

After six days, Jesus took Peter, James and John with him and led them up a high mountain, where they were all alone. There he was transfigured before them...
(verse 2)

Having read Matthew's account of this same event, there is something in the initial sentence here that strikes me afresh in Mark's telling.

Mark intensifies the fact that they were *"all alone"* (verse 2). Both he and Matthew use the very same Greek words to indicate the disciples were *"by themselves,"* but Mark adds the extra, intensifying word *"alone."* It's not a big change, but it jumps out to me this morning. There's an intentionality to it – Jesus chose that these three, all by themselves, alone, would have this experience of his glory. Further, it highlights they were cut off from other distractions. This is a time set apart, alone, with nothing else to intrude. There is also an intimacy, a sense of being drawn into a close circle with the curtain pulled back and heart revealed.

All of this is orchestrated by Jesus. He is the one who chooses and calls and leads to this place – alone. He does so because he wishes to make himself known.

My mind immediately goes to the other disciples. What about them? But before I go further (and count them second-best), I remember the Lord's words spoken on the eve of his death, spoken to us all: *"He who loves me will be loved by my Father, and I too will love him and show myself to him"* (John 14:21).

That high mountain location, then, is a picture of his heart for every single one of us. He wishes to show himself to each one, to make himself known. He chooses to take us aside, alone, to draw us into that circle of intimacy, revealing his heart. He desires that other distractions be put aside, that our sight might be focused solely on him. He wants us to know his glory.

Lord Jesus, I say "yes" – capture my sight with your glory.

I choose to take the time alone. Cut off other distractions. By your word and your Spirit, draw me into your presence. As you are transformed in my sight, transform me also with that sighting.

Amen.

Take time:

Two or three times throughout this day, set aside five minutes, alone, to focus on Jesus. As you do, know that it is his desire to show himself to you.

MARK 9:14-29

Jesus asked the boy's father, "How long has he been like this?"

"From childhood," he answered. "It has often thrown him into the fire or water to kill him. But if you can do anything, take pity on us and help us."

"If you can?" said Jesus. "Everything is possible for him who believes."

Immediately the boy's father exclaimed, "I do believe; help me overcome my unbelief!"
(verses 21–24)

"Everything is possible for him who believes."

Peter, James, and John have just been up the mountain with Jesus. They've seen an overpowering revelation of his glory and majesty, never to be forgotten. Meanwhile, down in the valley, their fellow disciples are confronted with a ministry need. A father has brought his young demon-afflicted son to them for deliverance. They've successfully responded to such needs before (6:7), but here and now they draw a blank.

Clearly this father has faith, at least enough to bring his son in the first place, hopeful for rescue. But the disciples' inability to provide any relief must have left him winded, wondering. Making matters worse, some teachers of the law, likely sent from Jerusalem to keep tabs on Jesus, have entered into a blistering debate with the disciples, probably further undermining whatever faith this distraught father still possessed.

Into this chaos strides Jesus. The assembled crowd sees him and is *"overwhelmed with wonder"* (9:15). The whole circumstance is about to be transformed with healing.

Mark enjoys telling this story, giving us much more detail than any of the other Gospels, including the interview Jesus has with the father. We simply wouldn't have known anything about this interaction apart from Mark. Clearly, he's got something he wants us to see. It turns out, what he's got in mind is the issue of faith. Matthew, in his telling, wants us to notice faith, too, but highlights it when Jesus debriefs afterward with the puzzled disciples, giving us his powerful statement about mustard seed-sized faith moving mountains (Matt. 17:20).

Mark's focus, instead, is on the dad. *"If you can do anything,"* he says, his faith battered by disappointment, *"help us."*

Jesus calls him up higher, rebuking his tentative *"if you can"* and calling him to full-throttled belief. *"Everything is possible for him who believes."*

I've heard people debate whether this long-suffering dad is an example of faith, or rather an example of quavering unbelief. What I know is that he is much more honest than I often find myself. It's as if he looks at both hands and discovers a small allotment of shop-worn faith in one, and at least an equal dose of invasive unbelief in the other, and in that moment, gives both to Jesus. *"I do believe; help me overcome my unbelief!"* It's full of such honest self-awareness. It is, in fact, a stance of faith itself, as he throws himself on the grace and mercy of Jesus.

The end result? His son was delivered. Oh, how faith must have grown. What prayers did he see powerfully answered thereafter as he pressed further into the stance of everything being possible in Jesus?

I'm sure heaven itself will tell that story.

Lord, I believe. Help me overcome my unbelief. For your name's sake. Amen.

Reflect:

What prayer or prayers are you currently praying that need this healthy dose of honesty? Take hold of both your hopes and your doubts and put them all in Jesus' hands. Then press into prayer anew.

MARK 9:30-37

Sitting down, Jesus called the Twelve and said, "If anyone wants to be first, he must be the very last and the servant of all."

He took a child and had him stand among them. Taking him in his arms, he said to them, "Whoever welcomes one of these little children in my name welcomes me; and whoever welcomes me does not welcome me but the one who sent me."
(verses 35-37)

As they were travelling through Galilee, Jesus for a second time tells his disciples (very clearly from our point of view) that he will be betrayed and executed, then rise again. The disciples failed to understand, but were afraid to ask anything further.

So, they launched instead into a debate about who among them was the greatest. It sounds juvenile to us, like schoolyard posturing, but apparently this wrangling for position was standard form in religious circles at the time. The Qumran community (source of the Dead Sea Scrolls) actually did an annual reckoning, ranking each member according to their relative worthiness, top to bottom. Ouch. The disciples were only following suit.

But Jesus calls them on it. Having arrived in Capernaum, sitting down together, he tells them that if they aspire to be first, they need to be last and serve the rest. It was a lesson Jesus would keep on teaching, right up to the very end, when at their last Passover meal he stripped off his outer clothing, wrapped a towel around his waist, and knelt at each disciple's feet, washing, cleansing, and refreshing. Even then, those rank-conscious disciples broke into an argument about who was greatest (Luke 22:24). Jesus' lesson was hard to learn.

On this occasion, in the house in Capernaum, Jesus pushes the issue with an object lesson. Taking a little child, he stands him among them so all could see. Children were considered of no significance, without rights and having no higher status than a servant. Indeed, in both Aramaic (which Jesus spoke) and Greek (which Mark writes) the same word doubles for both "child" and "servant." Taking the child, warmly, in his arms, Jesus says, "Welcome such a one." In essence he's saying, "I've just told you to be the servant of all – make sure you serve ones like this, who have no standing whatsoever – those you consider the lowest of the low. Serve these ones. Put yourself lower than the least."

He goes further. "Welcome them as eagerly as you would welcome me or my Father, because in fact that's what you'll be doing."

It's an ongoing challenge. Do we easily seek out the least? How willingly – how eagerly – do we welcome them? Do we have eyes to see those at the margin? Do we take the time?

As Paul puts it: *"in humility consider others better than yourselves . . . Your attitude should be the same as that of Christ Jesus"* (Phil. 2:3, 5). For Jesus himself lived this to the full. Indeed, he lived it to the end.

Lord Jesus, who are the ones you call me to serve? Give me eyes to see. Are there some, already staring me in the face, whose presence and need I've completely missed? Let me not be so focused on "important" things that I miss your fresh promptings today.

Reflect:

Take time in quiet prayer to reflect. Is there someone the Lord is prompting you to reach out to today with service or friendship or help or a listening ear? How will you respond?

MARK 9:38-41

"Teacher," said John, "we saw a man driving out demons in your name and we told him to stop because he was not one of us."

"Do not stop him," Jesus said. "No one who does a miracle in my name can in the next moment say anything bad about me, for whoever is not against us is for us. I tell you the truth, anyone who gives you a cup of water in my name because you belong to Christ will certainly not lose his reward."

In C.S. Lewis' book *The Silver Chair*, part of the Chronicles of Narnia series, Jill and Eustace have been given four signs to guide them on their quest to find the lost prince. Although the signs are given by the great Lion, Aslan himself, our heroes completely miss the first three of them. Everything now hangs on the fourth. *"You will know the lost prince . . . by this, that he will be the first person you have met in your travels who will ask you to do something in my name, in the name of Aslan."*[2]

When that request finally comes, it's on the lips of a man of whom they are deeply suspicious (is he bewitched, or is he in his right mind?). They are thrown into perplexing quandary – is he the prince or not? Yet he has spoken the name "Aslan." He's taken the Lion's name on his lips. It's the sign, sure and clear.

---

2   C.S. Lewis, *The Silver Chair* (Harmondsworth: Penguin Books, 1974), 29.

Lewis highlights the fact that fellow-followers of Jesus may turn up in unexpected places, from unexpected backgrounds. They may not look anything like what we had assumed. Indeed, they may make us slightly uneasy.

John, the disciple, had his own criteria for discernment. He states it simply: *"He was not one of us."*

How often is that our own criteria, too? Is this person from our own trusted circle? Do they agree with our theology at all points, especially those distinctive ones that are near and dear to our own hearts? Do they share our values regarding style of worship, political perspectives, use of money, priorities for ministry, level of education, and social ethics? Putting it simply, are they our kind of people?

Jesus seems to have a different standard entirely. Ultimately, it seems to be the one that Lewis puts forward: Do they embrace the name of the Lord?

Jesus implies that someone doing a miracle in his name is on his side. Likewise with the one who mundanely offers a cup of cold water, when done in his name. Not that the act of merely enunciating Jesus' name is a formula for salvation or sanctity. Rather, Jesus is speaking of life-motivation that is truly anchored in him, spilling forth into acts of service and ministry for the Kingdom that ring true with his lordship.

But the question remains, will we have eyes to see the heart of those who look so different on the surface? Will we be able to look past our own offended sensibilities and see the true heart of a sister or brother?

"Whoever is not against us is for us." In so saying, Jesus draws us into the circle alongside himself. And then, in the same motion, he draws in the other, also.

If Jesus can happily keep company with all who call on his name, we need to learn the same.

Lord Jesus, I ask your blessing this day on all those around me who are called by your name. I acknowledge I don't always have eyes to identify them clearly. Indeed, I confess there are some I have chosen to consider outside the circle. Right here and now, I bring them before you, asking your full blessing to be poured forth on them this day. Give me a heart to welcome them, also.

Reflect:

Who have you kept at arm's length, that you now see Jesus himself has welcomed? Ask the Lord to help change your attitude. Is there any other action you need to take?

MARK 9:42–50

"If your hand causes you to sin, cut it off . . . And if your foot causes you to sin, cut it off . . . And if your eye causes you to sin, pluck it out. It is better for you to enter the kingdom of God with one eye than to have two eyes and be thrown into hell, where 'their worm does not die, and the fire is not quenched.'"

(verses 43, 45, 47–48)

In literary terms, this passage employs *"hyperbole"* – excessive exaggeration to make a very strong point. Jesus is not encouraging self-harm, as if he wanted us to take destructive action against our own bodies. But his intent is equally impactful, if not literal. He is urging us to deal decisively with sin. He's pressing us to acknowledge those pathways in our lives, often well-trodden, that inevitably lead into disobedience. Spot them, he says, then cut them off. Do it without wavering. Put up barriers and "no trespassing" signs. Don't go there.

Such decisive action, by its very nature, involves curtailing some of our own freedom, limiting what we might well consider to be within our rights. But don't hold back. Deal with it, Jesus says.

Some of the "cutting off" and "plucking out" needs to occur in real-time, in our behaviours right here and now, right where we live. Some of the places we go can set us up for temptation – don't go there. Some of the "screens" that we watch can do the same. There are conversations we need to avoid, friendships we need to curtail, activities we need to sidestep because they lead us into sin every time. For each of us the list will be different, yet we know what the issues are.

But equally, much of the "cutting off" needs to happen within the confines of our mind, a location that is sometimes much more difficult to control, simply because it's hidden. The mind has great creative power for good, conjuring up images and remembrances. It can stew endlessly on circumstances and conjectures and problems and issues, teasing out angles, looking intently at every side. This creative freedom of the mind is a huge gift. But it's not always entirely helpful. Think of lust – stored images come to life, powerfully seducing us once again. Think of bitterness – memories that were long ago tainted by betrayal or slight, awaken to reactivate the pain, replaying a constant loop, again and again. Think of jealousy – all that competition and comparison, fuelled by our own insecurity, is rehashed, focusing laser-like on the one we find so threatening. And then there is the distraction of wrong-headed thinking (conspiracy theories or false teaching or "foolish stories that disagree with God's truth") that preoccupy the mind, leading us away from the Lord.

Such thoughts, roaming through our minds, can be slippery things to *"cut off."* But Jesus not only gives us the command, he stands by ready to give aid. Paul tells us to *"take captive every thought and make it obedient to Christ"* (2 Cor. 10:5). The image is helpful. Any unruly thought or memory or wrong-headed distraction can be arrested, as it were, and delivered to the feet of our Saviour himself. We submit it to him for obedience.

This act of *"cutting off,"* whether in our behaviour or in our thinking, may need to happen time and again. But the obedience of doing so is part of the process itself. And the One who calls us is eager to strengthen us in the task. Praise his name.

Lord Jesus, I hear your command. I know you are speaking to me. In my actions and in my thinking, I choose to "cut off" anything that is leading me into sin. By your Spirit, do your good work in me. Amen.

———————

Reflect:

Is there an activity or behaviour that needs to be *"cut off"* in your experience? Is there a pattern of thought or memory that needs to be *"plucked out"*? Talk to the Lord about it. Bring it all to his feet.

MARK 10:1-12

They said, "Moses permitted a man to write a certificate of divorce and send her away."

"It was because your hearts were hard that Moses wrote you this law," Jesus replied. "But at the beginning of creation God made them male and female. 'For this reason a man will leave his father and mother and be united to his wife, and the two will become one flesh.' So they are no longer two, but one. Therefore what God has joined together, let man not separate."

(verses 4–9)

Weighing in on issues of divorce can create problems. Certainly, John the Baptist discovered as much. Condemning Herod for his unlawful actions in marrying his brother Philip's wife, Herodias, led to John's arrest and subsequent beheading. Divorce is a tense issue. Likely the Pharisees, in raising it with Jesus, were hoping he might get into similar hot water.

For us, too, it's a fraught issue, tapping into biblical controversy and relational pain, plus the need for much grace, forgiveness, reconciliation, healing, and peace. Some, reading this now, know the depths of that reality all too well.

But it seems the central issue in Jesus' teaching here focuses not so much on the debate about divorce, but rather on the goodness of marriage. In raising their question, the Pharisees hoped to provoke a debate on the rationale and justification of divorce. But

Jesus in a sense brushes it all aside and instead heads into a closer look at marriage itself.

Marriage is hardwired into creation. When Jesus says that *"at the beginning of creation God made them male and female,"* he's not emphasizing the obvious distinction between the sexes, but rather setting us up for the one-flesh unity that results as these two distinct beings come together. What a marvel. God dreamed this up. How amazing. Creation itself presupposed this surprising union.

Where once each individual had a primary allegiance to parents, now that primacy is with a spouse. Previously, there were two separate single lives. Now there is one single united life. The two have become one flesh. It's expressed in the sexual relationship (wonderfully), but there's more. There is an interweaving of time and possessions and commitments and goals and hopes and dreams and challenges and on and on. It's all God's idea, woven into the very fabric of creation, right from the start.

When I got married in my mid-thirties, I'd been waiting a long time! One of my favourite wedding pictures was taken informally by a friend just outside the church doors immediately following the ceremony. I've got huge joy (and relief!) on my face as I spontaneously throw my arms wide to embrace my bride, oblivious to our friend clicking his shutter right at that very moment. All these years later, it's a slice of life I treasure! It captures the goodness.

Two final things need to be said. First, there will be painful moments along the way where divorce does indeed tear into this created fabric. Wonderfully, our God is not only Creator, but also Healer. Secondly, the same Lord calls some to a life of singleness rather than one-flesh union, without ever diminishing his promise to provide *"everything we need for life and godliness"* (1 Pet. 1:3)

All the while he's Creator, Healer, Provider, Sustainer. God is good, all the time. All the time, God is good.

Lord, I affirm marriage as your good gift. I lift my sights to those I know, whether married or single. I pray your power, peace, and joy for those seeking to faithfully live this oneness. I pray your healing grace for those who have suffered the pain of brokenness. I pray your abundant provision in everything for those who are single. In Christ's name. Amen.

———————

Pray:
Right now, pray God's rich blessing on friends who are married, friends who are divorced, friends who are single. Ask the Lord to meet each one this day, exactly where they are.

MARK 10:13-16

He said to them, "Let the little children come to me, and do not hinder them, for the kingdom of God belongs to such as these. I tell you the truth, anyone who will not receive the kingdom of God like a little child will never enter it." And he took the children in his arms, put his hands on them and blessed them.
(verses 14–16)

Children in Jesus' day had no status, no rights, no privilege, no pull. Therefore, it was completely counter-intuitive for the disciples to get their minds around the idea that *"the kingdom of God belongs to such as these."* This is a statement of sheer grace. If the Kingdom truly *"belongs"* to them, it cannot be on the basis of achievement or merit or inherent worth. Rather, it's pure gift.

Upon reflection, this is always the case, whether entering the Kingdom initially or living in it as an ongoing resident. It's not our accomplishments which give us the right of access. We don't rack up status on the basis of a stellar track record. It's never maturity which guarantees our position, nor longevity, nor pedigree of any kind. It's not gifting or skill or usefulness or ability. Not knowledge or wisdom or insight or learning. The Kingdom comes as pure gift – always. Life in the Kingdom continually has this character. We get into trouble whenever we place our confidence in anything other than the gift of Jesus himself.

But Jesus' statement also includes an insight about receptivity. What does it mean to *"receive . . . like a little child"*? Well, what have you seen? Here's what I've seen: If I offer a child something they perceive as valuable, they're all smiles, eagerness embodied, reaching out, ready to touch and handle and hold and possess – no hanging back. Not at all. It's just sheer joy, delight, trusting, and embracing. They enter right in, valuing the gift, accepting it wholeheartedly.

I want to receive from my Lord's hand, just like that.

Lord Jesus, thank you that you have been pleased to give me the Kingdom. It is pure gift, all of grace, never to be earned. What can I say, but "thank you," with all my being. I choose to receive it with delight. To enter in fully. To joyfully submit to your Kingdom rule.

This day, keep my eyes open to all you have given. May it be.

Keep track:
Today, be like a child and receive with delight the gifts of the Kingdom – every gift the Lord gives. Make a tally. Write them down. Try not to miss one of the gifts given to you. And give thanks for each one.

MARK 10:17-31

*Jesus looked at him and loved him. "One thing you lack," he
said. "Go, sell everything you have and give to the poor, and
you will have treasure in heaven. Then come, follow me."*

*At this the man's face fell. He went away sad, because
he had great wealth.*
(verses 21–22)

———————

The look in Jesus' eyes and the words in his mouth seem sharply divided. His eyes have deep love for the rich man kneeling before him, yet his words give an incredibly difficult, seemingly harsh, requirement. The look and the words appear to clash.

But on reflection, the love in Jesus' eyes tells us clearly the motivation for the words. Indeed, Mark is the only Gospel writer who adds this detail. Matthew tells us the man is *"young,"* and Luke tells us he's a *"ruler,"* but only Mark prefaces Jesus' command by telling us of the love in his eyes.

The insight is significant. The command (*"sell everything you have and give to the poor"*) isn't a hoop to jump through, proving his spiritual stamina and worth. Indeed, immediately previous to this, Jesus has expressly welcomed children into his presence, pointedly declaring that the Kingdom belongs to those who, like children in his day, have no rights or status of their own. We can never earn the Kingdom. It must simply be received. But, it is possible for our hands to be so full of other things that reception is thwarted.

That's the case for this *"rich young ruler."* The *"one thing"* he lacks, bottom line, is to *"follow"* Jesus. But he needs a radical break from his riches in order to be ready to do so. Those riches, left where they are, create an immovable impediment (like the eye of a needle for a camel). That reality is made clear by his immediate response to Jesus' instruction. He's come, intently desiring assurance of eternal life in the coming age. That's his goal. Apparently, it's what his heart desires. But when Jesus requires him to let go of the "stuff" of this present age in order to gain the blessings of the coming one, he balks. It's too much. He walks away sad.

Again, "giving it all up" isn't a means of earning eternal life. Rather, it's a necessary removal of hindrances that would keep this man from stepping fully into relationship with Jesus. *"Come, follow me,"* Jesus says, *and clear all this stuff out of the way to make it possible.*

So, making the application, it's not necessarily the case that everyone else needs to do the same. But before we all breathe a sigh of relief too heavily, let's actually consider whether if, like the rich young ruler, there is something hindering our own discipleship. Is money and its pursuit keeping our hands too full? How about career path and promotion and ambition? How about the pursuit of relationships with those who have very different priorities and values than does Jesus himself? What about excessive devotion to family traditions and guidelines and urgencies that dominate our schedule?

Bottom line is Jesus' call: *"Come, follow me."* Is anything inhibiting my response?

———

Lord Jesus, thank you for the love in your eyes. Thank you for your words of command. Give me eyes to see and ears to hear. Amen.

———

Reflect:

Is there anything inhibiting your discipleship today? What will it take to set it aside?

MARK 10:32–34

"We are going up to Jerusalem," he said, "and the Son of Man will be betrayed to the chief priests and teachers of the law. They will condemn him to death and will hand him over to the Gentiles, who will mock him and spit on him, flog him and kill him. Three days later he will rise."

(verses 33–34)

"I set my face like flint" (Isa. 50:7). This phrase from Isaiah's prophecy of Messiah keeps coming to mind as Mark portrays Jesus' determined, relentless progression to the cross. He knows where he's going. He knows what's coming. Yet, he perseveres, eyes on the goal, never diverting.

Jesus is centre stage, *"leading the way"* (10:32), the disciples following in his wake, with both astonishment and fear. The NIV translation indicates two separate groups, but Mark's text more likely speaks simply of the disciples alone. Did they sense Jesus' focused determination even before he spoke? Is that what stirred their emotions? The tension builds.

Then Jesus speaks. This is now the third major prediction, in as many chapters, of his approaching fate, each time emphasizing rejection and suffering and death (8:31–32, 9:31). Here, for the first time, Jesus states explicitly where this will all transpire – it will be in Jerusalem, the geographic centre of all things for Israel. It's Matthew who later records for us Jesus' heartaching lament over the city: *"O Jerusalem, Jerusalem, you who kill the prophets and stone those sent to you . . ."* (Matt. 23:37). Mark simply tells us that with determination he headed there, always knowing what was coming, never turning aside.

But the other thing Jesus makes clear for the first time is that there will be representatives of the full breadth of humanity involved in his rejection and execution. The Son of Man – who is the Christ and the Son of God – will be condemned to death by both Jews and Gentiles. It will include both the religious authorities and the secular. It will be those who have ethnic affiliation and those who don't. It will include those privileged to receive revelation written in history and in scripture, and those who have simply received the knowledge of God from what has been created. The full range of humanity will symbolically raise their hands in condemnation of the One who created them. As John would later reflect:

"He was in the world, and though the world was made through him, the world did not recognize him. He came to that which was his own, but his own did not receive him" (John 1:10–11).

Yet he pressed on. Knowing where he was going, he pressed on.

He did so, for the joy set before him. Each time Jesus predicts his death, he concludes with triumph. *"And after three days rise again"* (8:31). *"And after three days he will rise"* (9:31). *"Three days later he will rise"* (10:34). Simple. Succinct. Bursting with hope.

As the old preacher used to say, *"It's Friday, but Sunday's comin'!"*

———

Lord Jesus, thank you for your relentless progression to the cross – for me. Thank you for your willingness to endure rejection by the hands of those you came to save. Thank you for submitting yourself to death. Praise you that you triumphed over it. Praise your name.

———

Give thanks:

Throughout the day, pause to remember his persistence, and give thanks.

MARK 10:35-45

Jesus called them together and said, "You know that those who are regarded as rulers of the Gentiles lord it over them, and their high officials exercise authority over them. Not so with you. Instead, whoever wants to become great among you must be your servant, and whoever wants to be first must be slave of all. For even the Son of Man did not come to be served, but to serve, and to give his life as a ransom for many."
(verses 42–45)

The disciples, intensely, are jockeying for position. James and John have confronted Jesus with a self-serving request, namely prime positions (as perceived by them) in the Kingdom. They've rightly understood that the Kingdom is the true reality. They have true faith that Jesus is Lord. They've got it right that this future is certain. But they want to work it for their own advantage, locking in their own pre-eminence.

The other disciples, hearing about it, are indignant, not on principle, but for fear of missing out. Why didn't they think of this first? Ask and you will receive, right? What if those Sons of Thunder end up squeezing them out?

But Jesus turns the whole discussion on its head, defusing all its rancour and competitive angst. The Kingdom's not that way, he says. Kingdom greatness looks entirely different. Having position and status and authority is not what it's about – rather, taking the lowly position of servant, indeed slave. That's what counts.

A short time later the disciples would have an unforgettable image emblazoned on their minds as Jesus knelt before them, towel-wrapped, washing their grimy feet, an image rivalled only by the subsequent sighting of Jesus immobilized on the cross. Such service becomes the lifeblood of the Kingdom. Only on its basis are the gates of the Kingdom opened wide. Such service becomes the marching order for all who enter in.

So, what Son-of-Man-like act will I engage in today? What temptation to recognition and status can I push aside, willingly stepping down to a lower position? What rights must I hold loosely in order to live Kingdom-minded? Whose grimy need will I take in hand, serving like Jesus?

———————

O dear Jesus, Lord of the Kingdom, please, please give me the opportunity today to be like you. Give me eyes to see it. And when it arises, however unexpected it may be, give me boldness to look less-than, to come down, to set aside, and to serve. May this attitude be in me that also was, and is, in you.

———————

Eyes open:
Watch for a Christ-given opportunity to serve today, as a servant. Determine now you will embrace it when it comes, whether big or small.

MARK 10:46-52

A blind man, Bartimaeus (that is, the Son of Timaeus), was sitting by the roadside begging. When he heard that it was Jesus of Nazareth, he began to shout, "Jesus, Son of David, have mercy on me!"

Many rebuked him and told him to be quiet, but he shouted all the more, "Son of David, have mercy on me!"

Jesus stopped and said, "Call him."

So they called to the blind man, "Cheer up! On your feet! He's calling you." Throwing his cloak aside, he jumped to his feet and came to Jesus.

"What do you want me to do for you?" Jesus asked him.

The blind man said, "Rabbi, I want to see."

"Go," said Jesus, "your faith has healed you." Immediately he received his sight and followed Jesus along the road.

––––––––––––

This is the only time in Mark's Gospel that anyone addresses Jesus as *"Son of David."* The only other time the title is used is by Jesus himself, posing a theological question while he was teaching in the temple during the week before his crucifixion: *"How is it that the teachers of the law say that the Christ is the son of David?"* (Mark 12:35). In asking the question, Jesus implies that they've understood rightly – the Christ is, indeed, Son of David. Which then makes blind Bartimaeus very insightful indeed. He is one of only a very few people in Mark's Gospel who actually has eyes to see who Jesus is. And he's blind!

Having understood Jesus' identity, he presses forward with the correct response. *"Son of David, have mercy on me!"* he shouts. In some ways, blind Bartimaeus had an advantage. He very clearly knew his need. No question on that score. Jesus will later ask him directly, *"What do you want me to do for you?"* The answer is obvious, at least to Bartimaeus – *"Rabbi, I want to see,"* he says, simply and directly. His need is clear.

But the need also made him desperate. If there's any possibility of receiving sight, he wants it. So he cries out. The crowd rebukes him. He cries out the louder.

And his request is theologically sound. *"Have mercy on me!"* he pleaded. In crying out like that to Jesus, he laid bare his own need. In crying out, he declared with the whole of his being that Jesus is able. With his cry, he threw himself – without reservation, without safety net – on Jesus' compassion and love, trusting the Lord would act, knowing he had no other hope.

Even before his healing, Bartimaeus saw more clearly than most. I choose to stand side by side with him, acknowledging my need, crying out to Jesus, throwing myself on his mercy.

Jesus, Son of David, have mercy on me!

Pray:
Make this your prayer throughout this day. Pause often. Pray it in submission to his lordship. Pray it as you acknowledge specific needs.

MARK 11:1-11

Many people spread their cloaks on the road, while others spread branches they had cut in the fields. Those who went ahead and those who followed shouted, "Hosanna!"

"Blessed is he who comes in the name of the Lord!"

"Blessed is the coming kingdom of our father David!"

"Hosanna in the highest!"
(verses 8–10)

As I started into this passage this morning, the simple heading in my Bible, "The Triumphal Entry," shot through me with a thrill of excited anticipation. Yes! The King is coming!

Which must have been exactly what the crowd felt that day. Certainly, they expressed it with hearts and hands and voices. They spread cloaks and laid branches in the roadway, a royal carpet for the king's procession. They commandeered phrases from the Psalms, shouting them in acclamation and welcome. And they got it right – exactly. This was indeed the One who would save, completely. Hosanna (Save!) nailed it! He comes in the name of the Lord, with his full authority and anointing – truly! In him David's Kingdom finds its fulfilment, from that time on and forever – yes! What anticipation. What truth.

And yet, they missed it. Presumably many of these were the very ones who, just days later, would shout, "Crucify him!"

The irony, of course, is that the voices mix. The cry "Save!" overlaps with the cry, "Crucify!" The One who comes is the One who dies. The establishment of the Kingdom comes on the back of the cross. And the pathway of the King is the pathway of suffering and humiliation.

Hosanna, yes. Hosanna in the highest. Blessed is he who comes.

Lord Jesus, you knew. As you approached Jerusalem, you knew. You set your face for that place. You received the acclamation, rightly, yet you pressed on to your goal.

The glory of triumph comes through the cross. It is there that "Hosanna" rings the loudest.

Praise you, my King.

Reflect:

Take time to voice your own praise. Give thanks to the One who has come. We see the full story. Rehearse the signs of the King's glory. Let Hosannas ring.

MARK 11:12-19

On reaching Jerusalem, Jesus entered the temple area and began
driving out those who were buying and selling there. He over-
turned the tables of the money changers and the benches of those
selling doves, and would not allow anyone to carry merchandise
through the temple courts. And as he taught them, he said,
"Is it not written:
'My house will be called
a house of prayer for all nations'?
But you have made it 'a den of robbers.'"
(verses 15–17)

Wow. This story has become so familiar to me that I am in danger
of missing its dramatic violence. Not this morning. I am caught by
it, and somewhat troubled.

Jesus is strong, decisive, opinionated, and very physical.
Imagine the havoc. He strides in and, by force of personality and
strength of arm, begins to turf people out of the building. Heading
straight to the tables loaded with coins, he flips them over, sending
silver skipping across the surface of the floor, with money changers following, scrambling to retrieve their horde before themselves
being ushered out the door. Jesus similarly dispensed with the
dove sellers' benches, overturning and scattering them, with doves
flying and proprietors howling. He commandeered the central
thoroughfare, disallowing the movement of merchandise. And in
the midst of the ensuing chaos, he shouted out his indictment. The

temple was meant to be a house of prayer for all nations, but they had made it a robbers' den.

And did they hear that note of ownership in Jesus' voice as he passionately cried out *"My house"*? In the midst of their rage, did they feel conviction? As they scrambled to retrieve their "stuff" did they acknowledge the accusation in the label *"robber"*? Had they considered the temple's purpose was diminished by the size of their own enterprise, that a boisterous marketplace was antithetical to a house of prayer?

And at its root, did they catch the sense of generous hospitality in his yearning that the temple be a venue *"for all nations"*? By moving in tables and bird cages and money boxes and sheep pens had they realized they were squeezing Gentiles out? For, if they had looked around, they would have recognized that the clamour of their merchandizing was carried out in the "Court of the Gentiles," the one place in the temple precincts that non-Jewish seekers were allowed to venture. In the very fabric of the temple architecture was a provision for those who were as yet outside the circle, being reflective of the heart of Jesus himself who had come *"to give his life as a ransom for many"* (Mark 10:45). The full extent of that term *"many"* would not be clear until his sacrifice was made on the cross, but shortly thereafter it would spill forth in the command to *"go into all the world and preach the good news to all creation"* (16:15). Included in that *"many"* – captured in that *"all"* – were Gentiles, as well as Jews.

That's why he cleared the space. Yes, it was condemnation of religious life that had become as fruitless as a barren fig tree. Yes, it was a rebuke of misguided spiritual leaders. But at heart it included this commitment to provide a place *"for all nations."*

A place for you and me.

———

Lord Jesus, I stand in awe of your passion and strength. I marvel at your commitment to clearing out the clutter and providing space and place for all. I praise you that the same passions led you to the cross. All of it to the Father's glory. All of it for the sake of those who were lost. Praise you. Thank you.

Reflect:

Has anything in your own experience grown cluttered? Does anything need to be realigned with the Lord's heart and purposes? Ask him. Listen. Respond.

MARK 11:20-26

"Have faith in God," Jesus answered. "I tell you the truth, if anyone says to this mountain, 'Go throw yourself into the sea,' and does not doubt in his heart but believes that what he says will happen, it will be done for him. Therefore I tell you, whatever you ask for in prayer, believe that you have received it, and it will be yours.
(verses 22–24)

"Have faith in God." Move mountains. This scripture is so familiar, but I'm not sure I've ever fully believed it. The promise is so expansive, I think I've simply put it on the shelf.

But this morning it comes alive. This is Jesus' promise, sure and clear. I've been reflecting on the father of the demon-possessed boy back in Mark 9. *"I do believe,"* he says. Then, pressing forward, he says, *"Help me overcome my unbelief,"* asking Jesus to rescue him out of the doubt that lingers in his heart. It's a good prayer. It fits here, since the call is to ask without doubt clouding the heart, but simply believing.

So, Lord Jesus, help me. I need the lingering doubt to be removed so it no longer clings to this promise, dulling its edge. Rescue me in my unbelief!

Dear Lord, help me step into this teaching, finally, fully, here and now. I want to take it off the shelf, not leaving it there any longer, but rather embracing its fullness.

These words are spoken as Jesus and his disciples pass by a newly withered fig tree, cursed by Jesus the day before because of its unfruitfulness. His words, spoken in faith, produced this fulfilment. If the fig tree is object lesson number one, then the Mount of Olives, on which they are currently walking, provides object lesson number two. Apparently, from the mountain's heights, the Dead Sea itself actually comes into view, far away to the east. *"I tell you the truth,"* Jesus says, *"if anyone says to this mountain, 'Go throw yourself into the sea,' and does not doubt in his heart but believes that what he says will happen, it will be done for him."*

The sight of the fig tree stretches faith. The sight of that mountain and sea stretch it all the further.

Lord, I want to be stretched. I want to have doubt removed. I want to fully believe that what I pray will indeed be answered . . . by you.

Now comes the practicum. I have several prayers I've been praying, as yet unfulfilled. I've been trusting, but doubt has been niggling. I take in hand that father's prayer once again: *"I do believe . . . help me overcome my unbelief."*

Lord, I choose to reframe each of these prayers as mountain-moving ventures. I lift my eyes up, yes, to the mountain, but then out to the sea beyond, believing that you yourself will intervene to move the distance.

And as I pray, believing, I keep crying out for your help: overcome my unbelief. I submit it to you, Lord. This isn't my work after all. It's all yours.

Reflect:

What prayer of yours needs to be reframed as a mountain-moving venture? Grab hold in faith. Submit any lingering doubt to the Lord. Pray believing. Watch for his answer.

MARK 11:27-33

*Jesus replied, "I will ask you one question. Answer me, and I
will tell you by what authority I am doing these things. John's
baptism – was it from heaven, or from men? Tell me!"*
(verses 29–30)

The NIV translation at this point inserts an exclamation mark
after Jesus' final statement. Mark, writing in Greek, didn't have that
variety of punctuation – but the NIV accurately captures the tone.

This is a confrontational moment. The *"chief priests, the teachers
of the law and the elders"* gang up together and come to Jesus with
a very in-your-face question. Jesus has just cleared the temple,
an act of extreme condemnation of the current status quo. These
religious leaders, anger seething, now ask their very pointed questions, fully barbed: *"By what authority are you doing these things?
And who gave you authority to do this?"*

In the midst of his own anger (accurately captured by that
exclamation mark!), Jesus' brilliance shines forth. A direct truth-
ful answer ("My authority comes from God, my Father") would
simply be denied and then used as further accusation against him.
So Jesus puts back in their face their own previous rejection of
divine authority expressed in the ministry of John the Baptist. To
use a recurring theme of Mark's Gospel, they have had eyes but
failed to see, and ears but failed to hear. Indeed, the failure has
been rebellion. Further truth from Jesus' lips would only be met by
further blindness and deafness and hard-heartedness.

Where do we locate ourselves in this story? I find myself cheering Jesus on, glad for his brilliant confrontational response to these unyielding opponents. I rejoice that these foes are themselves put on the spot and that Jesus so clearly sports the upper hand.

But do I fully embrace his authority in my own life? Do you? When he strides in and overturns the status quo of my own experience, do I submit to his authority, looking for his further direction? Or am I in danger of getting my back up, balking at redirection, kicking against his intervention, or simply ignoring the commanding presence of his voice? May it not be.

"All authority in heaven and on earth has been given to me" (Matt. 28:18). That statement at the end of his earthly ministry sent his disciples into a lifetime of obedience. Gladly I, too, join them.

––––––––––

Lord Jesus, I acknowledge your authority in all my life. I submit to your lordship. I bow my knee. Be honoured, O Lord. Be glorified.

––––––––––

Reflect:
What active step can you take today to acknowledge Jesus' authority in your life?

MARK 12:1-12

"At harvest time he sent a servant to the tenants to collect from them some of the fruit of the vineyard. But they seized him, beat him and sent him away empty-handed."

(verses 2–3)

The centre of this parable has to do with the sending of the son, the heir. The rejection and violence that the tenants visit on him, killing him and casting him out, is a picture of the coming crucifixion of Jesus – powerfully prophetic.

But the theme that catches my attention this morning is the vineyard owner looking for fruit. He expects to share in the harvest – he expects to taste the bounty.

Coming on the heels of Jesus' encounter with the fig tree, looking for fruit but finding none, this part of the story stands out. The servant who comes to collect the fruit is sent away *"empty-handed."* It's just like Jesus approaching that fig tree – *"when he reached it, he found nothing but leaves"* (10:13).

This is an indictment on Israel at the time – the Lord expected fruit, but found none. The leaders of the day had focused so strongly on the external aspects of spiritual life (prayer on street corners and ceremonial washing and proper foods and tassels on garments and tithes of herbs and sabbath restrictions, etc.) that they missed the heart of the matter – they'd missed true devotion to the Lord himself. Indeed, the true nature of their hearts was exposed when Jesus appeared in their very midst and they refused to even acknowledge him. Worse yet, they conspired against him.

The Lord was looking for obedience, but their hearts were hard. He was looking for devotion, but he found distraction. He was seeking Kingdom fruitfulness, but found only barrenness. He came for the harvest, but was denied.

Such expectation fills his heart still. He comes looking for fruit. It's what he longs for. It's the very reason he chose us. *"You did not choose me,"* Jesus said, *"but I chose you and appointed you to go and bear fruit – fruit that will last"* (John 15:16). The apostle Paul embraced this same longing, praying for his friends in Colossae that they might bear *"fruit in every good work"* (Col. 1:10). Indeed, the Father himself puts in his hand, actively tending our lives, so that fruit may multiply – *"every branch that does bear fruit he prunes so that it will be even more fruitful"* (John 15:2).

He's waiting for harvest.

So, Lord, do your work. Tend the vineyard. Prune this branch. I yield to you my life that it may yield to you a harvest.

Reflect:

What fruit is the Lord tending in your own life? Where is he wanting to see harvest? How can you more fully yield to his plan?

MARK 12:13-17

But Jesus knew their hypocrisy. "Why are you trying to trap me?" he asked. "Bring me a denarius and let me look at it." They brought the coin, and he asked them, "Whose portrait is this? And whose inscription?"

"Caesar's," they replied.

Then Jesus said to them, "Give to Caesar what is Caesar's and to God what is God's." And they were amazed at him.
(verses 15–17)

I love Jesus' insightful brilliance. I love the fact that he sees right through their carefully sprung trap. I love watching as he skillfully evades incriminating himself, but at the same time gives a profound piece of instruction regarding godly interaction with the authorities of this world.

"Give to Caesar what is Caesar's and to God what is God's." Ultimately, of course, it's all God's. When it's clearly the right thing to submit to governing authorities, we do it because the Lord himself calls us to do so. The Lord is our chief motivation. By submitting to government, we submit to him.

The problem comes when the authorities of this world are actually in conflict with the authority of our Lord. The Apostles encountered this a number of times in the book of Acts. *"We must obey God rather than men!"* Peter fearlessly declared (Acts 5:29). They held their ground and paid the consequence, being flogged as a result (Acts 5:40). Many of them subsequently paid with their lives. We, too, may be called to pay the price.

But sometimes the lines are not so clearly drawn. *"Give to Caesar what is Caesar's and to God what is God's."* We can so easily get this mixed up. Indeed, sometimes it calls for very careful discernment to weigh and determine.

We found ourselves in such a situation with the COVID-19 pandemic. Restrictions on personal freedoms were instituted by governments in different constituencies to different extents. In some places, restrictions were also placed on church gatherings. That raised questions. Was it right to submit or was it right to rebel? Was this a sphere of Caesar's authority or was it one that belonged solely to our God?

Such an issue needed to be weighed thoughtfully before the Lord – committed believers would come to different conclusions. But along with careful weighing, there was also the need to examine one's own heart. Which phrase rings loudest in our soul: "my rights" or "godly submission"? If, during the pandemic, we balked at keeping other health guidelines mandated by government, like mask-wearing, it might be that our bottom line was simply a stubborn unwillingness to submit.

Such issues continue. Press into Jesus. Seek his perspective both for current affairs and current state of heart. Giving to Caesar and giving to the Lord both involve submission. So, submit. Follow his lead, honour authority, be bold, live with grace, love those who see things differently. In all these ways, give to God what is God's.

Lord, in the midst of a world that so often fails to embrace your values, give me ears to hear your direction. Grant me boldness to submit to you always. Grant me willingness to submit to those you have put in authority. Grant me wisdom to see clearly when their directives conflict with your own. Grant me strength to live the conviction. Amen.

———————

Reflect:

Look around in your own context. Are you holding back on anything you owe Caesar? Are you holding back on anything you owe God? What are the points of conflict? How will you respond?

MARK 12:18-27

Jesus replied, "Are you not in error because you do not know the Scriptures or the power of God?"
(verse 24)

The Sadducees had the Scriptures, the very revelation of God, but actually didn't accept it all. And even what they did accept, they didn't fully embrace. They had narrowed the scope of the Scriptures to the first five books of the Old Testament, the Pentateuch, the books of Moses. On that basis, they felt justified in rejecting any belief in the resurrection or angels or spirits.

Jesus challenges this theological disbelief by drawing solely on the Scripture they themselves affirmed, quoting the word of the Lord spoken to Moses at the burning bush, *"I am the God of Abraham, the God of Isaac, and the God of Jacob."* In so doing he refutes their mocking assertion that there is no resurrection. *"He is not the God of the dead, but of the living"* (verse 27), Jesus says. Of course.

Had the Sadducees been debating the issue of angels, Jesus could have similarly challenged their viewpoint. He might well have quoted any number of events from the Pentateuch, including Abraham's conversation with the Lord and his messengers regarding Sodom (Gen. 18-19), Jacob's dream of a stairway reaching to heaven (Gen. 28), the angel of the Lord encountering Moses at the burning bush (Ex. 3), and the angel who led the people of Israel out of Egypt (Ex. 14). The Sadducees had blinders on. They didn't take seriously the revelation they had been given.

Therefore, they cut themselves off from God's power. They reduced life to the natural, eliminating the supernatural, avoiding mystery, and thereby avoiding encounter with the living God.

How often do we do the same? We forget our God intervenes with power beyond the natural, fully able to transform impossibilities into the freshly possible. How often do we stop short of believing? How often do we neglect to truly embrace what we know the Scripture teaches?

O Lord, may you put your finger on my own disbelief, especially when I can't even see it for what it is.

Surprise me with clear-sightedness from the Scriptures, challenging my assumptions and drawing me to deeper faith.

I repent of the blinders I've adopted, influenced by the ordinariness of the world around me. I choose to open my eyes wide again to your truth, that I may be sure of what I hope for and certain of what I cannot yet fully see.

Help me, O my Lord.

Reflect:
Is there a circumstance in your life in which your faith has blinders on? If so, repent. Put it in the Lord's hands. Then embrace again the full truth of Scripture, and watch for the power of God.

MARK 12:28-34

"The most important one," answered Jesus, "is this: 'Hear, O Israel, the Lord our God, the Lord is one. Love the Lord your God with all your heart and with all your soul and with all your mind and with all your strength.' The second is this: 'Love your neighbour as yourself.' There is no commandment greater than these."

(verse 29–31)

The scribes had scoured the Old Testament scriptures and counted 613 commandments flowing out of them. The question then presented itself: Of all 613, which is the chief? Which best captures the essence of the whole?

The rabbis loved debate, so they eagerly plunged into this discussion. Rabbi Hillel, who lived just before Jesus, weighed in: "What you yourself hate, do not do to your neighbour; this is the whole law, the rest is commentary. Go and learn it." An interesting insight. But the debate continued.

So, one of the teachers of the law, noticing Jesus' thoughtful and insightful answers to other debated themes, asked him the question: *"Of all the commandments, which is the most important?"* (verse 28). While Matthew portrays this as another "test," Mark portrays the scribe as being absolutely sincere in his inquiry. He really wants to know.

So, Jesus responds. He brings forth two commandments from the Old Testament upon which all of the others hang. It's not that

155

the rest are to be disregarded, but rather that these two give the heart and soul and essence of all the rest. It's interesting that Paul will later grab hold of this same theme – *"love"* – and say that every other accomplishment amounts to nothing if this one thing is absent (1 Cor. 13). In essence, that's Jesus' point.

He directs it first toward God. *"Love the Lord your God with all your heart and with all your soul and with all your mind and with all your strength."* Love of God is the foundation for the whole of life.

I remember this commandment coming alive for me in university days. I'd grown up in a faith-filled Christian home and been nurtured in a Bible-believing congregation. My roots were deep and faith was real. But this foundational commandment went further and touched my heart. Love, of course, is more than emotion, more than a feeling. It involves action and obedience and commitment. But somehow the affections of the heart hadn't been highlighted in my younger days. So, this commandment opened that door, inviting me to embrace the Lord with *"all"* – what an absolutely expansive word. Nothing is left out. The whole of my being is included. Love like that, Jesus says. Yes.

And then, of course, there is the overflow of love to those around me, some of it easy and some of it so difficult. I am to love others as I love myself, having their back, wanting their best, speaking well of them, or holding my tongue. Washing feet. Serving like Jesus. Laying down rights. Embracing humility. Seeking their good.

I can never love my Lord as fully as he has loved me, but I can extend that love to those around me. To love others, then, completes my love of God himself.

"Love the Lord your God with all . . . Love your neighbour as yourself."

Lord, thank you for your command that invites me into the fullness of deep, committed, obedient relationship with you. Thank you that you stretch me more deeply in human relationship, giving of myself beyond what I otherwise would. You have poured out your love into my heart by the Holy Spirit whom you have given – by that same Spirit empower me to love in return. To Jesus' glory. Amen.

Reflect:

What is one new action you can take today to love God with all? What is one new situation in which you can love another like you love yourself?

MARK 12:35-40

While Jesus was teaching in the temple courts, he asked, "How is it that the teachers of the law say that the Christ is the son of David? David himself, speaking by the Holy Spirit, declared:

'The Lord said to my Lord:
"Sit at my right hand
until I put your enemies
under your feet."'

"David himself calls him 'Lord.' How then can he be his son?"
(verses 35–37)

Mark starts his Gospel by making it absolutely clear who he is writing about: *"Jesus Christ, the Son of God"* (Mark 1:1). To us, these titles, *"Christ"* and *"Son of God,"* seem to logically fit together. But not so for the Jews of Jesus' day. They understood the "Christ" or "Messiah" to be the God-anointed one who would come as a great deliverer of God's people. Israel was currently oppressed by the Romans, so they yearned for the time when the Christ would come in deliverance.

But they didn't expect he would be God himself. That was outside the box, completely beyond their expectations, not fitting any categories they had previously imagined. Although the Father had heralded this truth over Jesus from heaven at his baptism, people missed it. He spoke it again on the mountain of Transfiguration, saying, *"This is my Son, whom I love"* (9:7), but only Peter and James and John were privileged to hear, and it's not clear whether they fully understood. Even demons have cried out that Jesus is "Son of God," but others seem oblivious.

It's true that the title "son of God" is used in the Hebrew scriptures for kings and Israel itself, but Mark means us to hear it fully loaded.

So, Jesus now prods his listeners to open their eyes wider. He pushes them to reconsider their assumptions. Yes, he implies, the Christ will come in the line of King David himself. Yes, in that sense he will certainly be David's son. But what does it mean that David, the greatest King in Israel's history, actually calls him "Lord"? Doesn't that imply something more? This is the name that is used throughout the Hebrew scriptures for Almighty God himself. It's a weighty title. Why does David use it?

Jesus simply leaves the question hanging. It's meant to unsettle his hearers' assumptions. He wants them to take a second look.

That second look will ultimately lead them to the cross. That's where the veil gets pulled back. That's where the wonder comes clear. The Son of David is indeed the Lord. The One who is Christ is the One who is Son of God. Peter's clear-sighted declaration, "You are the Christ" (8:29), led Jesus to point his disciples to that coming cross, the place where, as "Christ," he would suffer and give his life as a ransom for many. And the clear-sighted declaration of the Roman Centurion at the foot of that same cross revealed the other half of Jesus' identity – the One who as Christ cried aloud and breathed his last was "surely . . . the Son of God" (15:39).

Jesus, the Christ, the Son of God. Yes. Praise his name.

———————

Lord Jesus, I honour you as the Christ, the One who has come to suffer and die, to give your life as a ransom for many, to give your life as a ransom for me. In the very same breath, I honour you as the

eternal Son of God, the One through whom all worlds were created,
the One who is worthy of all honour and glory and power, both now
and evermore.

Lord Jesus, I honour you. Praise your name.

Worship:
Pause right where you are. Give him honour and praise. Rejoice
that he is Christ, come to save. Praise him that he is the eternal
Son, worthy of all honour. Praise him, for he is Lord. Pause several
times this day. Honour him as Christ. Honour him as Son of God.
Honour him as Lord.

MARK 12:41–44

Calling his disciples to him, Jesus said, "I tell you the truth, this poor widow has put more into the treasury than all the others. They all gave out of their wealth; but she, out of her poverty, put in everything – all she had to live on."
(verses 43–44)

There's an intentionality, as always, to Jesus' activity this day. He sits down opposite the treasury in the temple and watches. Many people come and go. Many offerings are deposited. But Jesus singles out one for the disciples to notice. Here's what we learn:

- No offering is too small. The size of this poor widow's contribution is miniscule. She might well have thought to herself, "Why bother? I have so little to give – in the scheme of things it will make no difference at all." But her offering counts. Little could she have known the impact those two small copper coins would make, reverberating down the centuries since. Indeed, much greater, more long-lasting, than any other gift that day. So, none of us have too little. Each has the possibility of giving lavishly.

- The value of the gift is determined by the Lord. If others had been paying such close attention that day, they certainly would not have singled out the woman's gift as the weightiest of the lot. All they would have seen, with close inspection, was the relative weight of coin deposited. But the Lord is able to see the gift in the hand and the motive in the heart. He alone sees the whole. The woman, with devotion and commitment, took her little and gave with a full heart. On the Lord's scale, it weighed heavily.

- Giving is meant to be sacrificial. When it comes off the top of wealth it makes little impact on one's soul. The gift, large as it may be, is hardly missed. The power of money remains intact. But giving that cuts into the bottom line, however big or small that line may be, expresses an alternate lordship. The Lord reigns, rather than money. Sacrifice expresses that fact.

- Giving also expresses trust. Trust in the Lord. As she deposited those coins in the treasury that day, the woman was throwing herself wholeheartedly on the Lord's provision. She had just given him *"all she had to live on."* She was relying on the Lord for her own need. We, of course, don't know her full circumstance. All things being equal, we are called to handle money wisely, caring for our needs and those of our family. But whatever the full story in this case, the woman was radically trusting God. Her story inspires.

- The Lord watches. This is one of the most profound things we discover in this story. Jesus sat to watch. He pays close attention. He values our actions. He values us. He sees it all – the gift, our heart, the sacrifice, our trust. If he collects our tears in a bottle (Ps. 56:8), counts every hair on our head (Luke 12:7), and numbers all our days (Ps. 139:16), then it is no surprise he knows our finances and weighs our gifts.

What was the woman's story subsequently? How did she survive that day? How did faith and life unfold? We don't know. But I'm certain the Lord does – she was in his sights.

Lord, this day I entrust my own finances to you afresh. Here they are. I lay them out. Show me how you want me to use them. Show me how you want me to give. I trust myself into your care, again.

———————

Ask:

Reflect on your current practice of giving. Consciously ask the Lord for his direction. Is there some new way he wants you to give? Listen. Watch. Be ready to respond.

MARK 13:1–31

"At that time if anyone says to you, 'Look, here is the Christ!' or, 'Look, there he is!' do not believe it. For false Christs and false prophets will appear and will perform signs and miracles to deceive the elect – if that were possible. So be on your guard; I have told you everything ahead of time . . .

At that time men will see the Son of Man coming in clouds with great power and glory . . .

What I say to you, I say to everyone: 'Watch!'"
(verses 21–23, 26, 37)

So, how will we know the Lord when he comes? Signs and wonders would have seemed a sure bet, but Jesus says, "Don't rely on them," for false Christs and prophets will have the power of deceptive miracles, ready-made. Be on your guard.

So, how will we know? When the time comes, how will we know it's really him? Jesus says the sign of his coming will actually be unmistakable. Our own eyes will see him coming on the clouds with great power and glory. Indeed, Revelation 1:7 tells us *"every eye will see him."* His coming will be obvious to all, not to be missed.

So, don't get over-anxious and drawn in by compelling miracles. Don't be swayed by seductive signs. Rather, wait and watch till every eye sees him. Then your own eye, seeing and believing, will reach out to embrace him as Lord. Yes!

But in the meantime, be patient. And trust. I think these are the implications flowing from his statement: *"I have told you everything ahead of time."* What he means, of course, is that he's told us everything we need, not necessarily everything we want. We'd like to know the day and the hour, but we won't. If we did, perhaps we'd feel we could plan ahead, take things into our own hands, and simply get ready when we need to.

Instead, he's told us enough to know he's certainly coming. Enough to know times will grow tough. Enough to know we need to be on our guard.

Which is to say, he's told us enough to cause us to simply trust, and in that trust, to wait patiently.

Perhaps that's why he ends this teaching with the single-word command: "Watch!" It's the stance of certainty and anticipation, but also of patient trust, with eyes on Jesus.

Even so, come Lord Jesus.

Dear Lord, thank you for the assurance I will recognize you when you come triumphantly in the clouds on that great day. My knee will bow. My tongue will confess. Oh, how I look forward – even so, come!

In the meantime, work patient trust in my heart. By your Spirit, teach me to be on guard. And capture my being with the anticipation and certainty and abiding trust ringing out from that command, "Watch!"

I choose to live with eyes on you.

Pray:
Throughout the day, remind yourself of the Lord's command: *"Watch!"*

In response, pray the simple prayer, *"Even so, come Lord Jesus."*

MARK 13:32-37

"No one knows about that day or hour, not even the angels in heaven, nor the Son, but only the Father. Be on guard! Be alert! You do not know when that time will come. It's like a man going away: He leaves his house and puts his servants in charge, each with his assigned task, and tells the one at the door to keep watch.

"Therefore keep watch because you do not know when the owner of the house will come back – whether in the evening or at midnight, or when the rooster crows, or at dawn. If he comes suddenly, do not let him find you sleeping. What I say to you, I say to everyone: 'Watch!'"

Throughout this chapter Jesus has been giving his disciples prophetic instruction about the coming destruction of the Jerusalem temple, an event that will take place within *"this generation"* (verse 30). But he's also been looking much further forward, toward the day when *"men will see the Son of Man coming in clouds with great power and glory"* (verse 26).

This is where he has his sights set in this final paragraph of the chapter, focusing on *"that day,"* using a common Old Testament designation that refers to the end of time. *"No one knows about that day or hour,"* he says, so don't try to calculate. *"Only the Father"* knows, so don't presume you can nail it down.

Instead, be ready, always. Mark uses three different Greek words to record Jesus' instruction. *"Be on guard! Be alert! . . . Watch!"*

The first is a word that refers to our physical eyes, using them as a metaphor for the whole of life. Live "with eyes peeled" – that's the sense. The second literally means to be sleepless, to stay awake. Don't doze off in the midst of your duty – stay engaged! And the last gathers all of this up in its command to "Watch" – it's the word that Jesus keeps using in the Garden of Gethsemane, asking Peter and James and John to stand with him in prayer, in the hour of his need. Yet they did the exact opposite, dozing off each time.

Practically, what does this mean? Certainly, we're allowed to get needed sleep – the Psalms actually tell us the Lord gives slumber to his beloved (Ps. 127:2). But Jesus' point is this: don't fall asleep on the job. Stay actively engaged. Serve like a faithful servant in a large household, effectively employed even when the master is absent. Like the owner of that large house, Jesus has given us each Kingdom callings, tasks to fulfill for his purposes. Some of them will be clearly identifiable as "mission" and "ministry," but some of them will be much more mundane. Indeed, the whole of life, whatever we do, is meant to be actively offered as service for the Lord himself. *"Whatever you do, work at it with all your heart, as working for the Lord . . . It is the Lord Christ you are serving"* (Col. 3:23–24).

So, rather than spending your time calculating when that day will arrive (which, Jesus says, is an impossible task anyway, since only the Father knows), expend your efforts in being vigilant for the Kingdom, eagerly engaging every energy to the glory of Jesus.

"Be on guard! Be alert! . . . Watch!"

Lord Jesus, I look forward to that day when you will come on the clouds with great power and glory, calling me to yourself. How good. What joy.

In the meantime, please strengthen me by your Spirit to engage with my whole heart and soul and mind and strength in the work you have given me. To your glory.

Even so come, Lord Jesus.

———————

Reflect:

What Kingdom work has the Lord given you for today? If you don't yet know, ask him. If you do know, how will you engage to the full?

MARK 14:1-11

Some of those present were saying indignantly to one another,
"Why this waste of perfume? It could have been sold for more
than a year's wages and the money given to the poor."
And they rebuked her harshly.

"Leave her alone," Jesus said. "Why are you bothering her? She
has done a beautiful thing to me. The poor you will always have
with you, and you can help them any time you want. But you
will not always have me. She did what she could. She poured
perfume on my body beforehand to prepare for my burial. I tell
you the truth, wherever the gospel is preached throughout the
world, what she has done will also be told, in memory of her."
(verses 4–9)

I have often heard people speak of a "scarcity mentality." That's
what this woman's critics are evidencing. They consider that the
spilled perfume is a significant portion of a very limited resource
that has now been expended on something as frivolous as anointing Jesus' head. "Think of all those poor, hungry souls who will
now be perpetually impoverished because of this waste! What
was the woman thinking? And how could Jesus receive it gladly?
Where's his sense of proportion and priority?"

There's a deep sense of hypocrisy in this griping. Interestingly,
Matthew tells us the critics in this case are actually the disciples
themselves (Matt. 26:8–9). Jesus reveals their hypocrisy by saying,
"The poor you will always have with you, and you can help them

any time you want." In other words, "Why haven't you done something already? Why aren't you doing it now? Nothing's stopping you." Their sudden concern for the poor is a sham. They're simply offended by the woman's extravagant act and they justify their offense by citing the poor.

But even if hypocritically asked, what about the disciples' question? Don't they have a point? John tells us that the woman is actually Mary, sister of Lazarus and Martha (John 12:3). Isn't her action wasteful, out of sync with the reality of need surrounding her? Shouldn't she have used this perfume differently?

This is where a "scarcity mentality" skews the equation. After all, the One Mary honours is the One who owns the cattle on a thousand hills. The earth is his, in all its wonder and totality. Indeed, he is the One who, with a word, out of nothing, called it all into being. There is no sense of scarcity when we're dealing with the King of kings and Lord of lords! If the poor are always with us, so is he, with resources available, without measure, if we will simply choose to combine them with our own commitment to sacrifice – a commitment like Mary's, a commitment like the poor widow's in the temple (Mark 12:41–44).

Ultimately, the disciples' griping question misses the point. Where is their own sense of proportion and priority? The Lord of all creation is right in their midst, and they've missed the opportunity on this occasion to honour and bless him. Mary didn't. She seized the moment. In so doing, beyond her own understanding, she prophetically anointed the Lord for burial, anticipating the cross, highlighting the expanse of his own lavish sacrifice – a sacrifice poured out on us.

———

Lord Jesus, I choose to follow Mary's lead this day and honour you with the resources you have entrusted into my hands. With heart

and hands and voice, with wallet and time, I choose to worship you.
Lead me by your Spirit. I look to you, my Lord.

Reflect:
In what tangible way can you honour the Lord this day with your
own resources (energies, time, money, gifts)? Offer it up. Honour
him well.

MARK 14:12-26

While they were eating, Jesus took bread, gave thanks and broke it, and gave it to his disciples, saying, "Take it; this is my body."

Then he took the cup, gave thanks and offered it to them, and they all drank from it.

"This is the blood of the new covenant, which is poured out for many," he said to them.
(verses 22–24)

Taking the chapter as a whole, with its swirl of intrigue and accusation and agonized prayer and violence and arrest and condemnation, this moment is like the calm in the eye of the storm. Like the wind blowing through the Red Sea, it exposes the bedrock revelation of the moment.

"This is my body . . . This is the blood . . ."

I imagine the disciples, wide-eyed and uncomprehending. Salvation history is unfolding with force and rapidity right round them and they don't quite see it.

Yet the silent drama surges forward. They take fractured pieces of the unleavened bread of Passover, place it in their mouths, chew, and wonder. Then, in Mark's telling, it seems they take the cup in hand, one after another, in silence, completing the rotation of the table before Jesus pronounces the explanation, intensifying the drama. *"This is the blood of the covenant, which is poured out for many."*

Such simple, familiar elements – bread, wine – yet infused with meaning from centuries of repetition at the Passover feast. Unleavened bread, made in haste, symbolically free from sin, is eaten alongside bitter herbs and the sacrificial lamb, all of it proclaiming the Lord's deliverance from the bondage of Egypt. The cup, identified by Luke as the cup *"after the supper,"* which in Jewish tradition was named the Cup of Redemption, highlights the Lord's mighty hand rescuing his people.

Jesus gathers up all that meaning and focuses it, laser-like, on his own impending death. Deliverance. Redemption. New Covenant. In the quiet before the storm, it comes clear.

Jesus, Saviour, here in this quiet I receive your revelation to my own soul. Thank you, Redeemer, for your sacrifice, breaking sin's bondage, setting me free. I receive. I eat. I drink. I give thanks.

Receive:
Take a moment to receive afresh this gift, made personal to you. Pause to hear him say, *"This is my body."* Receive it to yourself. Again, pause to hear him say, *"This is the blood."* Receive it personally. Give thanks.

MARK 14:27-31

"You will all fall away," Jesus told them, "for it is written:
'I will strike the shepherd,
and the sheep will be scattered'" . . .

Peter declared, "Even if all fall away, I will not."

"I tell you the truth," Jesus answered, "today – yes, tonight –
before the rooster crows twice you yourself will disown
me three times."

But Peter insisted emphatically, "Even if I have to die with you,
I will never disown you." And all the others said the same.
(verses 27, 29–31)

What a poignant sighting. We know what's coming. Peter, confronted by a little servant girl, will decisively deny ever knowing Jesus. And then he'll do the same, twice more. It's a painful future encounter, and the pain bleeds backward into this moment of bravado.

The thing that strikes me here so powerfully is that the Lord knew. Right in that moment, face to face with Peter, the Lord knew. He knew the fear and desperation and faithlessness that would grip Peter by the fire, and that would continue to control him, spilling from one act of disloyalty into the next. The Lord knew, and yet he didn't shame Peter into acting differently, nor did he reprimand him in advance, nor did he disown him. He just simply stated what was going to happen.

Indeed, it's not simply that he has knowledge about Peter. He knows that each and every one of the disciples will also fall way. And it's not just a realization that came to him in that moment. No. The Lord knew hundreds of years in advance when, by the Spirit, prophetic insight was given to Zechariah to announce:

"I will strike the shepherd,
and the sheep will be scattered" (Zechariah 13:7).

Indeed, it goes back much further. The Lord knew from all eternity.

And yet knowing, he himself maintains faithfulness. And grace. More poignantly, such knowledge is what compelled him to come in the first place. He came as Saviour to those who, in their own strength, could only ever prove faithless and failing.

He came for me. He came for you.

Once Peter heard that cock crow and was wakened to his senses, the profound weight of guilt and shame descended upon him, and the realization would have dawned: the Lord knew.

And in that knowledge was the beginning of hope.

Lord Jesus, thank you that from all eternity you have known me. You have known my need. You have known your plan to provide salvation. You have known the cost. You have known the grace in which I now stand. You have known. Praise your name.

Reflect:
Consider that for each moment of your life thus far, the Lord has known. The good and the bad. The obedience and the disobedience. The faith and the faithlessness. Put it all into his hands again. Thank him for his grace.

MARK 14:32-42

They went to a place called Gethsemane, and Jesus said to his disciples, "Sit here while I pray." He took Peter, James and John along with him, and he began to be deeply distressed and troubled. "My soul is overwhelmed with sorrow to the point of death," he said to them. "Stay here and keep watch."

Then he returned to his disciples and found them sleeping. "Simon," he said to Peter, "are you asleep? Could you not keep watch for one hour? Watch and pray so that you will not fall into temptation. The spirit is willing, but the body is weak."
(verses 32–34, 37–38)

"Stay here and keep watch." It's a simple request. Immediate. Straight-forward. In the hour of his need, this is the charge Jesus gives his closest friends – Peter, James, and John. One would think they would sense its weight. One would think they would apprehend the need.

But it seems they almost immediately dozed off. I imagine they were awake long enough to catch some of Jesus' prayer, sufficient to be able to report it later, so that it ultimately found its way into Mark's record. But then they slept.

Meanwhile, Jesus continued labouring in passionate prayer, agonizing with the Father, anticipating his coming sacrifice, yet submitting to the Father's will. His enduring commitment is once again affirmed, and then he retraces the several short paces to the place his disciples waited. There he found them, slumbering soundly.

It's at this point that the narrative begins to sound familiar. *"Are you asleep?"* Jesus asks. *"Could you not keep watch?"* It's as if we've been plunged into the living reality of the parable Jesus had just told at the end of the last chapter. In that story, the Master had gone away, charging his servants to *"keep watch"* (13:34). That phrase (representing a single Greek word) gets used three times in Jesus' parable, emphasizing the necessity of staying awake and keeping alert. Now that very word rings out again, three times over, right here in the Garden. *"Watch!"* Jesus says. As Master, he gives this charge to his own servants, to Peter, James, and John. But they miss its weight. They fail to engage.

Going further, Jesus' story had given a severe warning to the servants not to be found *"sleeping"* when their Master returns. It's that very word that is used here in the Garden, not once, but four times over, describing again and again the dozy response of this intimate circle of Jesus' friends.

This is the very scene from Jesus' story. The very thing he'd warned his disciples to take seriously. *Keep watch. Do not let the Master find you sleeping.*

Yet here it is, played out in the Garden. The very scene. These disciples, charged to keep watch, are instead found sleeping. What do I learn?

1) Failure to watch comes easily.

2) It can trip up even those most intimately connected with the Master.

3) Sleeping on the job disconnects us from engaging in the very work of Jesus.

4) But it's not the end! Grace gives second chances. Take it from these disciples who ultimately learned to persevere

and keep watch: James being martyred because of faithfulness; Peter apparently martyred, also, after faithfully preaching the good news of Jesus time and again, even in the midst of persecution; and John living into old age, exiled because of Jesus, but listening to the Master faithfully to the end (see the book of Revelation).

———

Dear Lord Jesus, strengthen me by your Spirit to keep watch. I want to engage in all the work you have for me. Keep me from distraction. To your glory. Amen.

———

Reflect:
What work has the Lord specially called you into for this present season? What might distract you? How can you faithfully keep watch?

MARK 14:43-52

"Am I leading a rebellion," said Jesus, "that you have come out with swords and clubs to capture me? Every day I was with you, teaching in the temple courts, and you did not arrest me. But the scriptures must be fulfilled."

(verses 48–49)

The voice of Jesus defiantly rises above the chaos crashing in upon him.

It's a tumultuous scene. Action runs fast and furious. Irony swirls all around. Judas, intimate companion to Jesus over these preceding years, is now his sworn enemy, a mercenary betrayer, yet targeting his Master with the kiss of friendship as he delivers him securely into grasping hands. The members of that mob are violently armed with swords and clubs, standing in sharp contrast to the pious religious leaders who have sent them. Mark lists them all – chief priests, teachers of the law, elders, those who have been set aside to lead in spiritual life. Now, instead, they unleash a flood of violent hostility.

Peter (identified for us by John in his Gospel), pulls out his sword and swings wildly, eager to disprove Jesus' prophetic word that he won't be able to stand firm but will instead flee the scene and disown his Master. In the process he lops off the ear of the high priest's servant. Mark, refusing to slow his narrative, doesn't tell us the extra detail, captured by Luke, that Jesus himself paused in the chaos to heal the damage.

Then all the disciples scatter, vanishing from sight.

The final scene, with unintended humour, features a young man who has followed Jesus to this crossroads, wearing only a linen garment which he now unceremoniously leaves behind in the grasping hands of the mob seeking to detain him. With deft twists and turns he squirms from their grasp. He escapes, but his garment doesn't. Generations of readers have identified Mark himself as this one now fleeing in the buff.

Rising above it all, the voice of Jesus rings out. He puts his finger on the cowardice of the religious leaders, those who wouldn't even personally venture into the veiled darkness of that Garden to trap him, let alone arrest him in the glare of the Temple's daylight. He himself had taught there, boldly and publicly, each day of the past week, continuing to make himself known, not backing away, engaging in the debate, wading through the hostility, speaking God's word.

Wasn't it clear? He'd not come to lead a rebellion. Rather he'd come to heal one. The scriptures foretold it. All of it must be fulfilled. The Lord himself will do it.

Lord Jesus, thank you for enduring all the chaos churned up by sinful humanity. Thank you for purposely stepping into the turmoil in order to rescue and redeem.

Reflect:

Take time to examine any turmoil that is currently swirling in your own experience. Bring it before Jesus, knowing he is not overwhelmed when things run riot. Entrust the details to him. Receive his deeply rooted peace.

MARK 14:53-65

*Again the high priest asked him, "Are you the Christ,
the Son of the Blessed One?"*

*"I am," said Jesus. "And you will see the Son of Man sitting
at the right hand of the Mighty One and coming on the
clouds of heaven."*

*The high priest tore his clothes. "Why do we need any more
witnesses?" he asked. "You have heard the blasphemy.
What do you think?"*

*They all condemned him as worthy of death. Then some began
to spit at him; they blindfolded him, struck him with their firsts,
and said, "Prophesy!" And the guards took him and beat him.*

(verses 61–65)

Mark started his whole account with this statement: *"The begin-
ning of the gospel about Jesus Christ, the Son of God"* (Mark 1:1).
Right from the start he's wanted us to be absolutely clear about
Jesus' identity.

But as we've seen throughout, Jesus' identity has remained
obscured to most of the human participants, despite Almighty
God calling out his identity from heaven (Mark 1:11, 9:7) and
demons shouting out his credentials repeatedly. Peter correctly
identifies him as *"Christ,"* yet rebukes Jesus when he begins to
indicate that, as Christ, he's heading to the cross.

So, it's startling that in this tense moment of his trial, the chief antagonist actually puts Jesus' true identity into words, framing it as a question. *"Are you the Christ, the Son of the Blessed One?"* Up to this point in the trial, Jesus has remained silent – *"as a sheep before her shearers is silent, so he did not open his mouth"* (Isa. 53:7). He has refused to dignify with a response the bogus accusations which have been flung at him.

But now he opens his mouth. The drum roll sounds. Our attention is rivetted. Mark has been telling us all along, but now Jesus himself puts it into words. *"I am."* Deliberately he uses the phrase that reverberates with the Divine Name. Those present can't miss it. The crackle of the burning bush is heard loud and clear.

"I am . . . And you will see the Son of Man sitting at the right hand of the Mighty One and coming on the clouds of heaven." He places himself in the very centre of Daniel's apocalyptic vision of *"one like a son of man"* coming with the clouds of heaven and entering into the very presence of Almighty God (Dan. 7:13-14). Jesus places himself squarely at the Father's right hand, wielding his full authority, enveloped in his full glory. It's what Mark has been telling us right from the start.

But the religious leaders can't bear it. Their eyes, failing to see, are blinded to the revelation. Their ears, failing to hear, are deaf to the divine truth.

The high priest cries out, *"Blasphemy!"* The assembled leaders raise their voices in condemnation. The guards take him away.

Jesus, the Christ, the Son of the Blessed One, is heading to the cross.

Lord, I say it clearly and deliberately, with all my heart: You are the Christ, the Son of the Blessed One. Honoured be your name. Blessed are you, who sit at the right hand of the Father. Praise to you who. will come on the clouds of heaven. Thanks to you who went to the cross.

Repeat:

In your prayers this day, choose to use this full title again and again: *Jesus Christ, the Son of the Blessed One.* Reflect on its meaning. Repeat it again. Praise him. Thank him. Honour him fully. Embrace his revealed identity.

MARK 14:66-72

While Peter was below in the courtyard, one of the servant girls of the high priest came by. When she saw Peter warming himself, she looked closely at him.

"You also were with that Nazarene, Jesus," she said.

But he denied it . . .

Immediately the rooster crowed the second time. Then Peter remembered the word Jesus had spoken to him: "Before the rooster crows twice you will disown me three times." And he broke down and wept.

(verses 66–68, 71–72)

———————

Peter's denial doesn't come in one decisive moment, but rather as a series of knee-jerk reactions. The servant girl poses her question so quickly and unexpectedly that Peter gives a gut response, turning aside the immediate threat, hardly even noticing that he's set feet firmly inside the camp of denial. His heart, pounding rapidly when the question ambushed him, calms now as he moves from the fire out into the entryway. The menace passes, but leaves behind a dull aching awareness that something is not quite right.

Meanwhile, the girl, not satisfied by Peter's disavowal, follows. She's sure he looks familiar. She can't contain herself. She speaks out again, this time drawing in those standing by. "He's one of them – I'm sure of it," she says. Again, without thinking, without even noticing, responding by default, Peter denies it.

Again, the racing heart. Again, the dull ache. Then relative peace – at least momentarily. But it doesn't last. The crowd has taken notice. They're listening to his speech. He doesn't sound like a native of Jerusalem. He must be from Galilee, they surmise, and someone yells out: "Surely you're one of that crowd, too – clearly you're a Galilean."

Now Peter's heart surges with dread. Faces are turning. Fear overwhelms. Before it's too late he takes matters in hand. He makes a scene, cursing up and down, swearing he'd never even met the man. "I don't know this man you're talking about!"

At that moment, the rooster crows. In Mark's telling, it's the second time. The other Gospels don't specify "twice," they simply mention the crowing. In either case, it's all just as Jesus had predicted. It's all just as Peter had sworn would never happen. Remorse crashes over him. He breaks down and weeps.

And so it all would have ended, were it not for the cross.

The cross spells sin forgiven, stains washed clean, the old gone and a new page begun. Because of the cross, the story is not over. Not for Peter, and not for us. Indeed, Peter, forgiven and redeemed, went on to faithfully serve the Risen Lord.

His story tells us there's more to the story for us, too.

Lord Jesus, thank you for the love and determination that took you to the cross, a love that provides forgiveness and new beginning, when all I could have expected was guilt and remorse, judgement and shame. Thank you for a saving love big enough to cover all my sin. Praise your name.

Reflect:

Remember a time when you, like Peter, felt trapped by the weight of your own failure and sin. Remember, but don't hang on to it. Place it all in Jesus' hands again. Know afresh his forgiveness. *"Do not call anything impure that God has made clean"* (Acts 10:15).

MARK 15:1-15

"Are you the king of the Jews?" asked Pilate.

"You have said so," Jesus replied.

(verse 2)

"King of the Jews." What an exalted title. Indeed, higher still is the designation *"King of kings"* and Lord of lords (Rev. 19:16). What honour! Yet, it is this title, *"King of the Jews,"* that comes first, for it emphasizes his abiding love for his chosen people, his commitment to the nation of promise, and the priority of his mission to the lost sheep of Israel.

How wonderful, then, that this title is used again and again in this chapter, indeed six times over. Mark, writing out the title each time, intends us to understand its depth of authenticity and significance. But, ironically, those who actually pronounce it here do so without that appreciation. At best, they speak it with skepticism. More often, it's with mockery and contempt.

Pilate himself enunciates it three times. Jesus stands before him, seemingly powerless and stricken, not like a king at all. Under the hands of the chief priests and teachers of the law he has already been mocked and beaten and spit upon. Royal honour is certainly not forthcoming from that sphere. So, as Pilate asks his question – *"Are you the king of the Jews?"* – it's with a tinge of skeptical bewilderment. How would anyone ever think to call this one "king"? But I wonder if he actually has more cynical reasons for using the title again and again. Is he seeking to shame the

Jewish people each time he speaks it out, putting them in their place? After all, such weakness in a king reflects badly on a nation. The dishonour heaped upon him spills over on to his people, if he really is "King." So Pilate pronounces the title, over and over, tweaking the religious leaders and the whole nation with each use.

His final insult comes with the written charge he causes to be emblazoned above Jesus' crucified head: "KING OF THE JEWS." It's not given in honour. It's given in scorn.

So, too, as the soldiers strike him and spit upon him, laughingly calling out, *"Hail, King of the Jews!"* It's derision and cruelty that fill their hearts, not tribute.

Even the chief priests and teachers of the law use the title as accusation, mocking him as he hangs on that Roman gibbet. They pair it with the title "Christ," daring him to come down from the cross so they might believe. But, as Jesus said beforehand, *"they will not be convinced even if someone rises from the dead"* (Luke 16:31).

Do you hear it? Throughout this chapter, the truth rings out. Those who proclaim it don't know it, but they've nailed it. He is "King of the Jews." "King of kings." King of us all.

Lord Jesus, you are King. I honour you as my Lord. I commit myself anew to your sovereign rule. I bend the knee. I give my allegiance. I take up my cross. Thank you that you took yours.

Reflect:
What could you do this day to tangibly express commitment to your King? Make a plan. Carry it out. To his honour.

MARK 15:16-20

The soldiers led Jesus away into the palace . . . and called together the whole company of soldiers. They put a purple robe on him, then twisted together a crown of thorns and set it on him. And they began to call out to him, "Hail, king of the Jews!" Again and again they struck him on the head with a staff and spit on him. Falling on their knees they paid homage to him. And when they had mocked him, they took off the purple robe and put his own clothes on him. Then they led him out to crucify him.

"I offered my back to those who beat me,
my cheeks to those who pulled out my beard;
I did not hide my face
from mocking and spitting." (Isa. 50:6)

The third of the Servant Songs in Isaiah (each being a prophecy of Messiah) foretells the mocking cruelty of the Roman soldiers. Like Pilate, they accurately name Jesus *"King of the Jews,"* but do so in scornful derision. Flaunting their power over Jesus' perceived powerlessness, like so many bullies and oppressors before and since, they sought to humiliate him in every way possible. They stripped him, setting his clothes aside, then re-clothing him in a discarded military robe. Its purple colouring suggested royalty, prompting gales of callous laughter. Cruelly, they twisted together thorny branches into a makeshift crown, roughly pressing it on his bowed head, piercing his flesh, spilling his blood. With overlapping voices they derisively called out their hollow praise – *"Hail!"* Wave upon wave of scorn broke over him. They struck him on the head with a staff, spitting on him, showing contempt – their saliva mingling with his blood, running down face and neck. They fell to their knees, paying mock homage with raucous voices, the cacophony of scorn and mockery and contempt filling the air.

All of this was prophesied long years in advance by Isaiah, under the inspiration of God's Spirit. If all Scripture is God-breathed (and it is) then the Son of God himself had breathed out these insights long before they ever took place. He knew exactly what was coming, yet he pressed on.

Indeed, the Son of God inspired the riveting words of the next verse also:

"Therefore have I set my face like flint" (Isa. 50:7).

He had determined, long in advance, that he would not turn back, that he would set his gaze on the cross and, with rock-like resolve, press forward.

So, when *"they led him out to crucify him"* his determination carried him. He did not turn back. This was why he'd come.

Thank you, my Saviour.

I praise you, Lord, for the determination that took you steadfastly to the cross. You endured the scorn and derision, the suffering and pain. I stand amazed. Thank you.

Reflect:

"Consider him who endured such opposition from sinners, so that you will not grow weary and lose heart" (Heb. 12:3). In what situations can Jesus' example strengthen you today?

MARK 15:21-32

Those who passed by hurled insults at him, shaking their heads and saying, "So! You who are going to destroy the temple and build it in three days, come down from the cross and save yourself."

In the same way the chief priests and the teachers of the law mocked him among themselves. "He saved others," they said, "but he can't save himself! Let this Christ, this King of Israel, come down now from the cross, that we may see and believe." Those crucified with him also heaped insults on him.

(verses 29–32)

There's an awful lot of concern expressed here over Jesus saving himself. *"Come down from the cross and save yourself!" "He saved others but he can't save himself!"*

Jesus' accusers clearly equate his position on the cross with powerlessness. How could he possibly be the Christ if he's still hanging on that gibbet? In their minds, any lingering doubt is removed. Their accusations are thrown against Jesus, but they're meant to bolster their own position. "We got it right," they think. "He can't be the Christ – look where he is."

Yes, look. The unforeseen wonder is that it was his purposeful intention to end up there. This is what it means for him to be *"Christ."* He came *"to seek and to save what was lost"* (Luke 19:10). He came *"to give his life as a ransom for many"* (Mark 10:45). Yes, *"he saved others,"* but now he will do it to the uttermost. He will give his own life as a sacrifice of atonement so that the rest of us might live, forgiven and redeemed. Indeed, if he saved himself now, all others would remain unsaved. Salvation is taking place because he refuses salvation for himself. The mission (and the glory) of the Christ is so very different than anyone anticipated.

Arrogantly, the chief priests and teachers of the law position themselves as adjudicators of spiritual truth. *"Come down now from the cross, that we may see and believe."* They have determined that this show of power would prove Jesus to be the Christ, not realizing that it is actually a showing of his power (and compassion and grace) that keeps him there – not realizing that were he to descend now from the cross, they would be choosing to believe in one who refused to complete the sacrifice necessary for their own salvation.

They didn't realize they themselves desperately needed a Christ who would stay on that cross.

The book of Acts will later tell us that in Jerusalem itself *"a large number of priests became obedient to the faith"* (Acts 6:7). Perhaps it included some of those who, here and now, are so strongly embracing such a faulty criterion for belief. They needed a radical turn around, a new understanding of their own need for a Saviour, and a radically refocused vision of Jesus himself, just like the Pharisee, Saul, would later receive on a Damascus Road, far from Jerusalem.

Our Christ saves by not saving himself.

Lord Jesus, thank you for staying on that cross for me. Thank you for enduring the mockery and suffering and scorn. Thank you for not saving yourself, but saving me.

Reflect:

Take some time to picture, in your mind's eye, your Lord hanging on the cross. Give thanks. It was for you.

Stop regularly during the day and do the same. Reflect and give thanks.

MARK 15:33-41

And when the centurion, who stood there in front of Jesus,
heard his cry and saw how he died, he said, "Surely this
man was the Son of God!"
(verse 39)

This is one of the anchor moments in Mark's Gospel. Right from the very start he's made it clear he wants us to know Jesus' full identity. He started with these words: *"The beginning of the gospel about Jesus Christ, the Son of God"* (1:1). The story he's unfolded since those opening words has sought to make that identity clear. He is the Christ. He is the Son of God.

Halfway through his story, Peter had his revelatory moment of perception. *"Who do you say I am?"* Jesus asked. *"You are the Christ,"* Peter responded (8:29). Simple. Direct. Clear. Succinct. It took half the story to get there, but Peter sees. That's the first anchor.

Of course, we're aware in the story that perception can be somewhat fuzzy, as when the blindman received healing, and initially perceived people like trees walking. Peter didn't yet see clearly. He didn't understand that the Christ must suffer and die. So he rebuked Jesus when he first mentioned it. But sight was breaking through.

Now, at the foot of the cross, someone else has a moment of breakthrough. No human participant in the story to this point has put the second part of Jesus' identity into words. The Father has declared it from heaven, both at Jesus' baptism and on the mount of Transfiguration. *"This is my Son, whom I love"* (9:7). The demons, through human voices, have repeatedly cried it out. *"You are the Son of God"* (3:11). But no person has declared it in their own right. Not till now.

What was it that tore back the veil, allowing the light of clarity to pierce through? It seems it was Jesus' death itself. This centurion would have been no stranger to death on a cross. He'd see it often. The cross was cruel, designed to break men and triumph over them, to exhaust and deplete them before death ever gripped them. This centurion had seen it. All strength and life would ebb away, ounce by ounce. By the end, the victim would simply fade into death, all power gone.

But not Jesus. Having hung on the cross all morning, then through the sun-darkened hours of early afternoon, his voice pierced the air, crying out from the cross. Mark simply tells us it was *"a loud cry"* (verse 37). But John tells us the words: *"It is finished!"* (John 19:30). Simple. Direct. Clear. Powerful. This was not the cracking whisper of the exhausted dead. No – there was the unmistakable sound of triumph in Jesus' voice. As he passed from this world it was as if he were the victor, springing an ambush on death, taking it by sudden surprise, wrestling it out the door.

The centurion heard it. Like nothing he'd ever heard before. The conviction dawned. Even though it was beyond full understanding, the words formed:

"Surely this man was the Son of God!"

Mark wants us to hear it, too. Surely.

Lord Jesus, your death clearly reveals that you are the all-loving, grace-bestowing, ransom-paying Son of God. Surely. Thank you. Praise your name.

Reflect:

Picture the cross. Reflect on these words: *"the Son of God, who loved me and gave himself for me"* (Gal. 2:20). Pause. Linger. Give thanks.

MARK 15:42-46

Joseph of Arimathea, a prominent member of the Council, who was himself waiting for the kingdom of God, went boldly to Pilate and asked for Jesus' body.
(verse 43)

We only hear about Joseph of Arimathea at this point in the story, and we never hear about him again. But he's in the spotlight long enough to inspire.

Each of the Gospel writers gives us different details about this man who appears so briefly. Mark tells us that he is a prominent member of the Council, the Sanhedrin, which had orchestrated Jesus' death. Mark had already told us that the Sanhedrin trial had unanimously condemned Jesus. Luke, on the other hand, tells us that Joseph himself had not given his consent to their decision, leading to the conclusion that for whatever reason Joseph had been absent from this decisive interrogation.

We get a sense of his spiritual devotion when both Mark and Luke tell us that he was *"waiting for the kingdom of God."* It indicates an orientation of life toward the things of God, yearning for something more, being anchored in the Scriptures and looking forward to the fulfilment of the Lord's long-given promises. Both Matthew and John inform us that at some point prior to this time his spiritual yearning had drawn him to Jesus and he had actually become one of his followers. But John gives us the additional insight that he did so secretly because he feared the Jews, namely the rest of his fellow leaders. So, Joseph has much at stake. He has an established, respected position among the religious elite, no doubt accentuated by an authentic and obvious spiritual devotion, but now complicated by the fact that he has fallen in with Jesus who has disastrously fallen out with the Sanhedrin itself.

His action then, as reported by Mark, is startling. He goes directly to Pilate, asking for Jesus' body, that he might give him an honourable burial. Under Roman law, an executed criminal lost all right to any honour whatsoever in death, and the body of the crucified victim was often left on the cross to rot and be scavenged by birds of the air. Even the possibility of burial could only be realized if permission was given by the ruling authorities. This was especially the case for the burial of someone convicted of high treason (such as one claiming to be a King), a burial which was on principle disallowed and required a special exemption.

In requesting Jesus' body for burial, then, Joseph ran the risk of being viewed in the same treasonous category as Jesus himself. He also risked exposing his devotion to Jesus to the other members of the Sanhedrin. As one who up to this point *"feared the Jews"* (John 19:38), this was an unlikely move. No wonder Mark tells us that he *"went boldly to Pilate."* He overcame fear, exposed himself to risk, and stepped forward, finally, with visible devotion to the one he had chosen to follow.

It's the only moment in Mark's Gospel that Joseph of Arimathea comes into view. But I'm so glad he does. His fear turns to courage, his timidity to boldness. He inspires us to do likewise.

All in devotion to Jesus.

———————

Lord Jesus, may you strengthen me by your Spirit to walk in increasing boldness as I follow you. May I, like Joseph, step forward, in

devotion to you, setting aside fear, not worrying about risk. All in
devotion to you.

Reflect:

Consider whether you have been living in fear and timidity in some aspect of your life. Ask the Lord for boldness to step forward.

MARK 16:1–8

"Don't be alarmed," he said. "You are looking for Jesus the Nazarene, who was crucified. He has risen! He is not here. See the place where they laid him. But go, tell his disciples and Peter, 'He is going ahead of you into Galilee. There you will see him, just as he told you.'"

Trembling and bewildered, the women went out and fled from the tomb. They said nothing to anyone, because they were afraid.

(verses 6–8)

This is where the earliest manuscripts of Mark's Gospel end. It's a cliff-hanger. Verses 9–20 seem to have been added by someone else later to fill out the resurrection account with details mostly familiar from the other gospels. But the shorter ending certainly focuses the sharp reality of the drama.

"He has risen! He is not here." What a shock – ultimately filled with joy unspeakable, but in the moment it is hardly surprising that these women were afraid. Terrified. They were face to face with the power of divine intervention, face to face with a *"young man"* who was clearly more than a man, announcing world-shaking news that would reverberate down through history. Yet in that moment, they were without the calming wonder of being face to face with Jesus himself.

That was yet to come. In Galilee. Just as he promised (14:28). But not yet.

So, whether Mark intended this abrupt ending, or whether his original ending has been lost, the stunning impact of the good news is here in all its shocking wonder. *"He has risen! . . . There you will see him . . ."*

It all comes down to the person and work and word of Jesus. What he has promised is always sure. The end of this story is guaranteed. The wonder, in the midst of fear, is already breaking in, reverberating from an empty tomb in angelic tones.

It moves us still. *"He has risen! . . . He is going ahead of you . . . There you will see him . . ."*

———————

Lord Jesus, Risen Lord, grip me, today, with the shocking surprise of your resurrection. The tomb is empty and everything is changed. Ready my heart to heed your call. Strengthen my will to follow as you go ahead of me this day. Give me eyes to see your presence. Praise you!

———————

Reflect:

When I was a kid in Sunday School, we used to sing a chorus that started like this: *"I serve a risen Saviour, he's in the world today . . ."* What difference will this truth make for you today? If this is indeed true, what events, meetings, or circumstances will be different as a result?

MARK 16:9-20

He said to them, "Go into all the world and preach the
good news to all creation."

(verse 15)

It seems clear that this whole final portion was not originally part of Mark's Gospel. It's not included in the most important early manuscripts and simply sounds different than the rest. It seems likely that the original ending to the Gospel was lost early and this summary section was added to fill it out. That being said, this portion draws on the witness of the other Gospels and piggy-backs on their authority.

That's particularly true for the verse I've highlighted above (16:15). This is the Great Commission from Matthew 28:18–20, but more focused, with different wording.

The heart behind it is identical – the very heart of Jesus himself who came *"to seek and to save what was lost"* (Luke 19:10). Up to this point, Jesus has been focused on the people of Israel. *"First let the children eat all they want"* (7:27), he'd said to the non-Jewish, Syro-Phoenician woman. But now, on this side of the cross and resurrection, he wants the good news to break out for all human-ity. *"Go into all the world,"* he says, that little word *"all"* being entirely expansive, as big as the whole cosmos. Don't hold back. Don't allow any corner to be unreached. Be propelled into each and every circumstance, to each and every person.

"Preach the good news to all creation." The word *"preach"* contains within it the image of a herald standing in the centre of town, crying out the news in a loud voice, clearly declaring an authoritative message.

This, of course, is literally what those first disciples did – think especially of the Day of Pentecost, and Peter at the Beautiful Gate of the Temple, and Paul in the heart of Athens. Such large-scale proclamations have continued ever since, right through church history, with Billy Graham in recent times as an outstanding example.

But it also happened in smaller settings: Stephen before the Sanhedrin, and Peter in Cornelius' house, and Paul speaking to a gathering of women at the riverside outside Philippi. And it happened more personally yet: Philip with the Ethiopian eunuch, and Paul with the Philippian jailer, and later before Festus, Agrippa, and Bernice.

It continues. Whether to large audience or small, the proclamation continues. We ourselves have opportunity, indeed calling, to step into it, too. Some are specially gifted for this task, proclaiming good news in such a compelling way. Others will simply spill it forth as they're able, not feeling particularly gifted, but knowing the reality of the calling. *"Go into all the world . . . to all creation"* is a task that requires all of us to engage. The glorious proclamation of good news is meant to go forth to all. Our own part may not seem like much, but it's part of that bigger picture.

As the Sunday School song from my childhood put it: *"Jesus bids us shine . . . You in your small corner, and I in mine."* May we live it. May we truly embrace our own part of *"all."*

———————

Lord Jesus, give me eyes to see my portion of "all." Give me boldness to step into it fully. Through my words and through my life, make your proclamation clear. Give me increasing joy in this wonderfully good news.

Reflect:

The calling is to *"all."* Reflect on your own sphere of influence. Ask the Lord to use you in the lives of one or two (or three or four). Begin to pray for them to receive good news. Step into the opportunities the Lord provides.

KEEP GOING

We've been on a journey through the scriptures with the intent of seeing Jesus more clearly.

Don't stop. Keep going. Keep reading.

Press on into John's Gospel – he has a completely different style, capturing many different events and teachings from Jesus' ministry. He was right there alongside Jesus through most of it, following closely and understanding himself to be *"the disciple whom Jesus loved."* He has a unique perspective.

Or backtrack to Matthew's Gospel and see how he handles many of the same stories and themes as did Mark. Most scholars feel Matthew had a copy of Mark's Gospel in front of him as he wrote, using that material, but also adding his own insights and remembrances – after all, he, too, like John, was a direct eyewitness as one of Jesus' own disciples.

Or skip forward to the Book of Acts and see how Jesus continued his ministry, in the power of the Spirit, through the lives of his Apostles and others. Or plunge into one of the letters written to the newly founded communities of believers (Romans or Ephesians or Philippians or one of the others) and see how the risen Lord Jesus was shaping their lives and interactions. Or fast-forward to the panoramic vision of the Apostle John in Revelation, focused on Jesus as the Victor – it's a powerful sighting!

Wherever you settle, keep eyes on Jesus throughout.

That's his intent. On the first Resurrection Sunday, as he walked with two disciples on the Road to Emmaus, Jesus looked back to the Old Testament scriptures and *"explained to them what was said in all the Scriptures concerning himself"* (Luke 24:27). If we were walking with him on the road right now, he would do similarly with the New Testament scriptures. They were written to focus on Jesus, to help us understand what it means to be *"in him,"* to give us greater vision of what he is continuing to do in the world around us, and allow us to see where the whole story is leading.

So, keep going. Keep reading. Don't stop. Know that the Holy Spirit has been given to lead us into all truth and to put the spotlight on Jesus himself.

Eyes on Jesus. That's the point. To his glory.

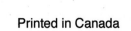
Printed in Canada